Laboratory Manual

The
SCHEMATICS

of

COMPUTATION

Vincent S. Manis
James J. Little

PRENTICE HALL, UPPER SADDLE RIVER, NJ 07458

Production Editor: *Kimberly Knox*
Produuction Supervisor: *Joan Eurell*
Acquisitions Editor: *Alan Apt*
Assistant to Acquisitions Editor: *Shirley McGuire*
Production Coordinator: *Donna Sullivan*

Printed in the United States of America

10 9 8 7 6 5 4

ISBN 0-13-834714-X

Prentice-Hall International (UK) Limited,London
Prentice-Hall of Australia Pty. Limited, Sydney
Prentice-Hall Canada Inc., Toronto
Prentice-Hall Hispanoamericana, S.A., Mexico
Prentice-Hall of India Private Limited, New Delhi
Prentice-Hall of Japan, Inc., Tokyo
Pearson Education Asia Pte. Ltd., Singapore
Editora Prentice-Hall do Brasil, Ltda., Rio de Janeiro

Contents

Preface

A fool ... is a man who never tried an experiment in his life.
— Erasmus Darwin, grandfather of Charles Darwin (1731–1802), letter

The Schematics of Computation shows our vision of computer science as a unified discipline based upon a relatively small number of concepts. Physics is about matter, energy, space and time; computer science is about algorithms, abstraction, and representations. The book uses these fundamental concepts to build object-oriented programming, evaluators, relational data bases, and inference engines, among many other concepts.

One who reads the book will grasp something of our vision, but the only way to understand anything is to go beyond reading to doing. Reading a book on cycling won't prepare a person for the Tour de France. In the same way, reading about computation is no substitute for direct exploration of the concepts.

Any experimental discipline operates by developing hypotheses, and then performing experiments to test them. Computer science is different from the traditional sciences (and even engineering), in which the scientist models a universe that already exists. Computers, programs, languages, and methodologies didn't exist until humans invented them. Once these tools were invented, investigators found that they had their own rules and behavior, and that many of the results were not at all what was expected. As in other sciences, experimentation is then used to test hypotheses about the constructs under study.

The results in computer science can often be useful. A new graph traversal algorithm can help lower the cost of constructing an integrated circuit; a new kind of user interface can help people with neural problems to control their world more effectively. This fact has often been held against computer scientists, pigeonholing us as mere tinkerers.

But even the act of writing and testing a computer program is itself a kind of science. The programmer must construct a model of some system in the real world in building a program, and must make sure that the program (and thus the model) in fact behaves in the way the real-world system does. Programmers must thus construct theories of the world, and test those theories by experiment.

These two kinds of computational experiments—those that test hypotheses and those that test programs—lead to an understanding of computation not as a large number of disparate languages, applications, and techniques, but as a universe in which a very small number of powerful concepts and methods can be used to build powerful tools and programs. This Laboratory Manual provides a set of experiments that lead the student to this realization.

Goals of a Lab

A traditional lab in computer science presents a problem, and then concludes with a one sentence exhortation such as "Write a program that solves this problem." The student then does something or other to attempt to solve the problem, and submits the result to an instructor, who then grades it on criteria such as how well it works or whether there are enough comment lines. What the student actually learns may or may not be what the instructor intended. The stated goal is to write a program to solve a problem; the goal of understanding the result is often not stated.

In our rethinking of computer science labs, we looked to labs in other sciences. In these labs, the student often reconstructs a pivotal experiment, or works with tools in order to understand them better. Goals and the steps the student must take to achieve those goals are clearly stated. Some labs (e.g., measuring the acceleration of a cart going down a ramp) are predominantly analytical; others (e.g., building a sweep circuit for a cathode ray tube) are predominantly constructive.

Our labs are designed to give a student experiential learning of the concepts presented in the book. We want students to learn the specific concepts presented. We also want students to learn the modeling and validation skills needed to build successful programs.

A student who does the labs in this book will gain experience in the phases of software development: design, implementation, and validation. (We do skimp on requirements analysis, which is too advanced for an introductory course.) Some labs emphasize analysis (students must read code and make modifications); others emphasize synthesis (students must write complete programs).

Structured Labs

Traditional computer science labs are *specifications of the result to be produced*. The lab handout describes the program to be produced, and gives perhaps a few suggestions about how to develop that program. A student may follow a path quite different from that the instructor is attempting to elucidate; a task the instructor has set in order to explore an algorithm might be implemented by calling an undocumented operating system procedure. The student might feel a sense of accomplishment at developing this solution, but that does not mean the student has mastered the point of the lab. And what of the weaker student? A person who can't even decide what to do first has little chance of producing a useful solution to the problem at hand.

The labs in this book are *specifications of a process to be explored*. Each lab describes a problem and outlines a strategy for solving it. The work the student does is divided into "Before the Lab" (analysis and design that must be done before using the computer), "During the Lab" (programming, testing, and exploration to be done at the computer), and "After the Lab" (analysis and wrapup to complete the lab). The labs guide the student through the process of design, implementation, and validation.

But what of creativity? The labs in this book are not mere typing exercises. Each requires the student to think through some fairly complicated concepts, and to write some non-trivial code, in order to reach the destination. We outline strategies, and sometimes procedure, module, and class specifications. The rest is up to the student.

Some of the labs in this book emphasize *writing* programs; others emphasize *modifying* programs. Students can develop their programming skills in two ways: our programs provide many models, and of course the code they write will provide valuable feedback on good and bad strategies. A student who completes all of these labs will have written several substantial programs, and will have studied many more, including working versions of:

- two Scheme evaluators (a substitution evaluator and a recursive Scheme evaluator that uses environments)
- a word-guessing game
- an Adventure game
- an object-oriented network simulator
- an inference engine
- tools for reading Extended BNF and generating sentences from EBNF grammars
- a relational database package
- a symbolic differentiation package
- an assembler and simulator for a hypothetical computer

We have found these labs to be a valuable tool in teaching the concepts in the text, and they form an integral part of any course that uses the book.

To The Student

Science is built up of facts, as a house is built of stones; but an accumulation of facts is no more a science than a heap of stones is a house.
— Henri Poincaré, *Science and Hypothesis*

We designed this Laboratory Manual as a way for you to learn the concepts presented in our book, *The Schematics of Computation*, and to give you the programming skills needed for success in the computing field. Each lab covers a topic from the book. In some, you will be writing programs; in others, you will analyze existing programs.

We believe that doing lab work is the *only* way to learn programming. By attacking these problems, you will learn the concepts thoroughly, and you will become a confident programmer.

Very few of the labs are specifically about Scheme. As we said in the book, we only use Scheme as a tool for studying computer science. Even so, we do provide advice on good Scheme programming practices.

Each lab has the following parts:

1. **Objectives**   A brief description of the concepts and skills this lab will teach you.
2. **Problem Description**   A description of the problem area the lab will investigate.
3. **Before the Lab**   Some pre-lab problems that get you started on the lab.
4. **Pitfalls**   Tips on techniques that will be useful in the lab, and traps to watch out for.
5. **Checkpoint**   A set of questions designed to test that you understand the problem carefully.
6. **During the Lab**   The steps you need to follow in the lab.
7. **After the Lab**   A set of problems in which you analyze the work you've done in the lab, compare and contrast different approaches, or apply what you have learned to a different problem.
8. **Deliverables**   A list of the products you will have produced in this lab, suitable for handing in to an instructor. (Sometimes you will create a printout for several related tasks.)

To do a lab, you will *start* with reading, *continue* with analysis and design, *test* your work at a computer, and *finish* by analyzing and putting together what you've learned. Make sure you read the **Deliverables** *before* you start working on the lab; that way you'll know what you're actually trying to produce.

Some labs have sections For Further Investigation, where you can attack related problems, or expand your solution in some way.

Even though the labs are structured in detail, you will still need to be creative to solve some of the problems. Organizing a large program is not an easy thing to do; our suggestions and instructions are based upon not only our experience as computer science teachers, but also our experience in using these labs with other students. Even though we strongly recommend you follow those instructions, there are still many places in each lab where you must still think carefully about how you are going to solve the problem.

We have carefully designed each lab to teach you some important concepts of computer science. As you do the lab, follow the steps carefully. Even though you might be tempted to explore other paths, experience has shown us that students have their hands full just in completing the lab. If you have time, you can always revisit the alternatives once you've finished the lab.

Acknowledgments

We must first thank the hundreds of students who have suffered with our preliminary versions of these labs. Their suggestions and comments have vastly improved the manual.

Our thanks for the labs here go to Don Acton, Carl Alphonce, Art Boehm, Craig Boutilier, Roelof Brouwer, Dave Forsey, Jason Harrison, Jason Holmes, Michael Horsch, Cedric Lee, Nick Pippenger, and Marko Riedel.

We are particularly grateful to Maria Klawe and Bob Woodham of the Department of Computer Science, The University of British Columbia, and to Judy Boxler and Habib Kashani, Department of Computer Science, Langara College, for their strong moral support and encouragement of this project.

Support for this project was also provided by the Department of Computer Science, The University of British Columbia, and by Langara College.

Lab 1
Getting Started With Scheme

Early programmers worked directly with the computer; they would enter instructions and data directly into the computer's memory, and observe the results in flashing lights and printouts. It was extremely tedious at the best of times, and much, much worse when a program had a bug in it. Modern programmers use a **programming environment**, a package of programs that help them not only to type in the program, but also to diagnose what went wrong when something goes wrong.

This lab is designed to give you some experience in using your programming environment. The details will vary depending upon the particular Scheme system you are using, as well as the operating system (DOS, Windows, Macintosh, OS/2, or UNIX, for example) you're using. The principles, however, remain the same.

WHAT YOU NEED TO KNOW

Read up to the end of Section 1.2. You will also need some information about your Scheme system and operating system, not to mention such practical details as where the computer lab is located. Your instructor will provide this information.

PROBLEM STATEMENT

Even though the details vary enormously, all Scheme environments give you:
- a **top-level**, a program that lets you type in Scheme forms directly, and displays their values
- a **text editor**, a program that lets you type in Scheme programs into a file, and then load them into the top-level

A Scheme top-level typically produces the dialogs shown in the book, such as

```
> (+ 2 2)
4
```

Scheme top-levels also can report error messages. The exact way this is done will depend upon the specific system. As with all programming environments, sometimes the error reports are misleading: the top-level reports the problem from its point of view, not the user's. Part of learning the programming environment is learning how to deal with errors.

Although a top-level is useful when you're trying out single forms, it is not suitable for typing in programs. For this you need a text editor, a program that lets you type in your program and then, when it is complete, enter it into the Scheme top-level (this process is known as **loading** the program into Scheme). Some Scheme environments include their own special editors. Others allow you to use the text editor of your choice.

BEFORE THE LAB

1. Evaluate by hand the following expressions.
   a. (- 4 9) $4-9 = -5$
   b. (* 3 9) $3*9 = 27$
   c. (+ 3 (* 5 4)) $3 + (5*4) = 23$
   d. (/ 7 2) $7/2 = 3.5$
2. Write a Scheme form that computes $3^2 + (2.75 - 4)/3 \times 2$. Evaluate the Scheme form using The Rules.

   (+ (expt 3 2) (* (/ (- 2.75 4) 3) 2))

1

CHECKPOINT

1. Translate $2 + 3 \times \sqrt{16} - 5$ into Scheme.
2. Evaluate (* (- 9 4) (+ 2 5)).
3. Does a text editor play any part in evaluating Scheme forms?

DURING THE LAB

1. Following the instructions you will be given, start up your Scheme system. Scheme has the ability to produce a **transcript**, a file containing a record of your interaction with the system. Start a transcript.
2. Things can go wrong. Type in each of the following "forms" (none is valid Scheme), and see what happens. Press the ⎡Enter⎤ key after entering each "form". (Your computer keyboard may label this key as ⎡Return⎤.)
   a. I like to program in Scheme!
   b. (+++ 2 3)
   c. (/ 5 0)
3. Type in the forms in part 1 of your pre-lab work. Check that the results match your expected ones.
4. Type in your form from part 2 of your pre-lab work. Check that the result matches your expected one.
5. Start up the text editor for your Scheme system, and type in the following form, *exactly as shown*, except for changing the first line so that it includes your name and other identifying information.

```
;;; «Your name goes here»
;;; Procedure for computing the volume of a sphere.
;;; Inputs:
;;;    radius is the radius of the sphere (must be a number
;;;    greater than or equal to zero to get a sensible result).
;;; Returned value:
;;;    the sphere's volume.
(define sphere-volume
  (lambda (radius)
    (*
      (/ 4.0 3.0)
      (* 3.1415926
        (* radius (* radius radius))))))
```

Save this file under the name sphervol.scm, and load it into Scheme. Evaluate each of the following forms:
   a. (sphere-volume 0.0)
   b. (sphere-volume 1.0)
   c. (sphere-volume 2.0)
If you are doing this lab on a home computer, you may be tempted to use a word processor such as Microsoft Word to enter your program, rather than the text editor provided with your Scheme system. Don't! A word processor is generally not a very good program editor.
6. Close the transcript, and produce a printout of the transcript and the file you created, sphervol.scm.

AFTER THE LAB

1. Joel User types in the following fragment of Scheme code to the Scheme top-level, and then presses the ⎡Enter⎤ key. What happens? Why? (Hint: how long will Joel have to wait for the system's response?)

   > (+ 2 2

2. Evaluating the two forms 6a.b and (/ 5 0) both result in an error message. In the book, we discuss the **syntax** and **semantics** of an error message. Which of these forms is syntactically incorrect? Which is semantically incorrect?

3. Under what circumstances should you use the text editor to create a form, rather than typing it directly into the top-level?

4. Evaluate each of the following Scheme expressions using The Rules, (Version 1, as given on page 21). *Be sure to show all your work.*
   - a. (+ 5 (* 4 9))
   - b. (* 6 (+ 2 4))
   - c. (/ 63 (+ 4 3))
   - d. (+ (/ 2 3) (/ 16 6))

DELIVERABLES

1. the printout from your Scheme session, and the listing of the file sphervol.scm
2. the answers to the problems you did after the lab

(1) Scheme waits until he closes the (parenthesis. & presses return again. It could potentially wait forever.

(2) 1st one is syntax. 6a.b isn't a recognized form.
    2nd is semantics; division by 0 is undefined

(3)

(4)

Lab 2
Evaluation in Scheme

Programming languages can be learned in one of two ways. Either you can learn a large number of special rules, or you can learn the general principles underlying the special rules. Because Scheme is a simple and consistent language, Scheme programmers can learn the general principles that underly it more easily than in many other languages. We have written a Scheme evaluator that works pretty much the way The Rules works. By experimenting with this evaluator, you will see how these rules help in determining the value of a Scheme form. You will also write and test a small Scheme program.

WHAT YOU NEED TO KNOW

Read up to the end of the discussion on procedures and definitions in Chapter 1 (Section 1.3).

PROBLEM STATEMENT

This lab consists of two parts. In the first, you will work with our special Scheme evaluator and observe carefully what happens during the evaluation of a form. In the second, you will build a Scheme program.

The Substitution Evaluator

The substitution evaluator is a program, written in Scheme, that behaves the way a regular Scheme system does. It asks you to type in a form (giving you a subst-eval> prompt), and then evaluates it for you. There are two big differences between the substitution evaluator and regular Scheme systems: first, the substitution evaluator follows the rules we covered in the book, whereas Scheme follows a set of more complex, but much more efficient rules (getting the same result); and, second, the substitution evaluator tells you when it performs each step. For any real problem, the substitution evaluator would produce far too much output; since our goal is to understand evaluation, the substitution evaluator is just right.

The Vintner's Problem

A winemaker has two large cylindrical vats of wine, and a collection of bottles of three different sizes: 3, 4, and 7 litres. The first vat has radius 5 metres and height 10 metres; the second has radius 4 metres and height 12 metres. (The volume of a cylinder is its height times the area of its base.) A litre contains 1000 cubic centimeters.

We need a program that computes the number of bottles of wine of each size that each of the two vats will fill.

BEFORE THE LAB

1. Evaluate, following The Rules, Version 2.0 (see the book, Page 47), the following expression:

   ```
   (* (sqrt 16) (- 12 (* 3 4)))
   ```

2. Write down the Scheme expressions (forms) that express the calculations you need to solve the Vintner's Problem.

3. Calculate the correct answer for the Vintner's Problem, so that you can check, in the lab, whether your program is operating correctly.

PITFALLS AND ADVICE

The computer scientist Richard Hamming once said, "The purpose of computation is insight, not numbers." The goal in the Vintner's Problem is not to get the correct answer (a pocket calculator can do that) but to create a program that is general enough to solve problems with different numbers. The calculator produces an answer; a program is a tool for computing answers.

You must use procedures and definitions in your solution, so that it is easy to change your program to work with different values. A good program will have some procedures that do general calculations (the volume of a cylinder, for example), and some forms at the end that apply these procedures to the specific data of the problem.

Make a chart showing the arguments and return values for each procedure, so that you can be sure you understand what each procedure is supposed to do. What you will end up with is a collection of definitions, some for the procedures you are using, and some for the particular numbers of the problem.

When you write your code, pay special attention to making the code readable. Choose your procedure names carefully, and include a comment at the beginning of each procedure that explain what it does.

You will need the Scheme primitive `ceiling` to compute the number of bottles from the volume—there can only be a whole number of bottles. `ceiling` takes a number and returns the smallest integer (whole number) greater than or equal to it.

CHECKPOINT

1. What rule (in *The Rules*) do you use to evaluate (*#{plus}* *3 4*)?
2. What does Scheme do when you evaluate ((lambda (x y) (* 2 (* x y))) 3)?
3. The vintner needs to compute the wine's price. The price is computed at 50 cents for the bottle, plus 1.5 cents per millilitre. Write a procedure that calculates the price for a given volume of wine (the last bottle may be only part-full).

DURING THE LAB

In many of the labs you will need to use Scheme code we have written for you; the substitution evaluator is the first of these programs. We provide a set of **goodies**; a goodie is a Scheme file stored on your system that supplies some procedures used in the labs. Most labs will require you to load a goodie file.

1. Load the substitution evaluator; it is contained in the goodie `subst.scm`. To start the evaluator, evaluate (subst-eval). To terminate the substitution evaluator, type in (stop). Start and stop the substitution evaluator.
2. Make sure you know whether you're talking to the substitution evaluator. Type (`ceiling 1.5`) to Scheme. Type (`ceiling 1.5`) to the substitution evaluator. Why do you get different results?
3. Type in the following forms, and see what the evaluator does with each:
   a. 5
   b. (+ 5 5))
   c. (* 4 (- 5 5))
   d. (* (+ 5 5) (- 3 1))
4. `subst-eval` can also handle lambda expressions. Try the following forms:
   a. (lambda (x) (* x 2))
   b. ((lambda (x) (* x 2)) 4)
   c. ((lambda (y) (* y 2)) 4)
   d. ((lambda (x y) (* y x)) 3 4)
   e. ((lambda (x) ((lambda (y) (* y x)) 3)) 4)
   (That last one is a monster!)
   A careful examination of the substitution evaluator's output will reveal that it goes through some unnecessary steps. Identify them.
5. Look back at the output you have obtained so far, and notice that operators such as + are evaluated as well. (+ evaluates to something that prints as {plus}: this is in fact the machine-language subprogram for adding numbers together.) In fact, every position of an application is evaluated.
   Test this by running the form ((lambda (f) (f 3 2)) *) Make sure you understand what is going on. Which of 2 and 3 is evaluated first?

6. Get a printout of your session, and put it aside.

7. Now try out your solution to the Vintner's Problem. You should do this in a fresh copy of Scheme. The easiest way to do this is to exit from Scheme *(be sure to get your transcript first)*, and then start it again. Type your program into a file (call it vats.scm), and save it. Then test it out. You should get the answers that you calculated. If it doesn't work, find out what's wrong, and modify it. When you have got everything right, get a printout of both the file and your Scheme session, and put them aside.

AFTER THE LAB

1. Go through your printout from the evaluation problems, and make sure that you understand what's going on.

2. Why did you get different results from typing (ceiling 1.5) to the Scheme top-level and to the substitution evaluator?

3. What are the unnecessary steps the substitution evaluator goes through?

4. Write (in longhand, or, even better, use a word processor) a brief explanation of the differences between the rules as shown in the book and what the substitution evaluator does.

DELIVERABLES

1. Your printouts: the evaluation session, a listing of the Scheme code for your solution to the Vintner's Problem, and the session where you tested it out.

2. Your answers to the After The Lab questions.

FOR FURTHER INVESTIGATION

A computer store calculates a cost for its computers according to the following formula:
- the base machine costs $1650.
- memory costs $20 per megabyte (million bytes).
- (hard) disk storage costs $0.75 per megabyte.

For example, a 16 megabyte machine with a 540 megabyte hard disk drive would cost $1650 + 16 × $20 + 540 × $0.75 = $2375. Write a Scheme procedure or set of procedures that calculates the total cost for a given computer configuration.

Deliverables: Two printouts: your Scheme code, and a session in which you test it.

Lab 3
Decisions

OBJECTIVES

Programming languages provide Boolean values for representing answers to Yes/No questions. Predicates are procedures that return Boolean values; conditionals allow us to choose between two forms depending upon a Boolean value. These tools allow us to build procedures that compute different values depending upon the argument values. In this lab, we will investigate Boolean values, predicates, and conditionals. We are now ready to write larger programs, so we will also see how to organize a programming project, and how to test code properly.

WHAT YOU NEED TO KNOW

Read up to the end of Chapter 1. Make sure you understand boolean values, predicates, and if, and, and or.

PROBLEM STATEMENT

The law office of Dewey, Cheetham, and Howe mails many letters to its clients. Each day, the office staff separates letters into bundles, each bundle consisting of n identical letters being mailed to the same city. What is needed is a program that computes the total postage charge for a bundle.

The Post Office charges according to the following formula:

$$p = f(d) \times g(w)$$

where d is the distance in kilometres and w is the weight in grams.

f is the distance factor, calculated according to these rules:
- less than 6 kilometres, 0.03
- 6 to 399 kilometres, $d \times 0.05$
- 400 kilometres and over, $20 \times \sqrt{d/400}$

g is a function that computes the charge for the weight, according to the the rules stated in the Exercises at the end of Section 1.4:
- less than 30 grams, 15 cents
- 30 to 49 grams, 17 cents
- 50 to 99 grams, 22 cents
- 100 grams and over, 1 cent for each 4 grams

In addition, the Post Office gives a volume discount (v); the more letters you mail, the lower the cost per letter. based on the following rules for mailing n letters. If n is
- less than 100, $v = 1$
- 100 or more, $v = n/100$

However, the volume discount is not available for overweight letters. If the weight is greater than 125 grams, $v = 1$ regardless of the value of n.

You will need to write several procedures.

PROCEDURE (weight-charge *w*)

ARGUMENTS
- *w* is the weight in grams

RETURNS
- the charge for a letter of this weight.

PROCEDURE (distance-factor *d*)

ARGUMENTS
- *d* is the distance a letter is being mailed, in kilometres

RETURNS
- the distance factor for the letter

PROCEDURE (overweight? *w*)

ARGUMENTS
- *w* is the weight of a letter

RETURNS
- #t if the letter is overweight, #f otherwise

PROCEDURE (volume-discount *n w*)

ARGUMENTS
- *n* is the number of letters being mailed
- *w* is the weight of each letter, in grams

RETURNS
- the volume discount for this mailing

PROCEDURE (total-cost *n w d*)

ARGUMENTS
- *n* is the number of letters being mailed
- *w* is the weight of each letter, in grams
- *d* is the distance the letters are being mailed, in kilometres

RETURNS   the postage required, in dollars

We have specified each procedure by describing the inputs and outputs expected. We will use this notation throughout the manual.

The total cost for a bundle is a product of volume, the cost based on weight, the distance factor, and the volume discount (if any). If we put the procedures described above together, we will get a program that computes this total cost.

The approach we took in specifying these procedures is called **procedural abstraction**: we divided the problem into tasks, and specified a procedure for each task. We *could* have just written this as one giant procedure, but the resulting code would be too complicated to understand and debug.

BEFORE THE LAB

1. Evaluate, following 𝕿𝖍𝖊 𝕽𝖚𝖑𝖊𝖘 Version 2.0, the following expressions:
   a. (define double (lambda (x) (+ x x)))
   b. (+ (+ (/ 39 11)(/ 39 11)) (+ (/ 7 2.0) (/ 7 2.0)))
   c. (define double-and-add
        (lambda (a b) (+ (double a) (double b))))
   d. (double-and-add (/ 39 11) (/ 7 2.0))

2. If you have not already done so, do Exercise 1-34. Call the procedure `weight-charge` (the solution at the back of the book calls it `postage`, but that's too general a name for this procedure in our expanded version).

3. Write some values of *w* that will thoroughly test `weight-charge`. Write down the corresponding values that `weight-charge` should return.

4. Write a procedure that calculates the distance factor.

5. Write some values of *d* that will thoroughly test your distance factor procedure. Again write down the value the procedure should return.

6. Write the `overweight?` predicate.

7. Write some values of *w* that will thoroughly test `overweight?`, and the expected results.

8. Write a procedure that calculates the volume factor, using `overweight?`.

9. Write some values of *n* and *w* that will thoroughly test your volume factor procedure, and the expected results.

10. Write a procedure that calculates the total cost to mail *n* letters of weight *w* grams a distance of *d* kilometres.

11. Write down a set of values of *n*, *w*, and *d* that thoroughly tests your total cost procedure, and the expected results.

PITFALLS AND ADVICE

Whenever you're asked to write some code, pay special attention to programming style. Make your code easy to follow, correct or change. Do not forget to test your code. Testing code is an important step where you discover the limitations and correctness of your code.

Moreover, you should indent your code as in the book. If you have an auto-indenting editor, use it. If not, follow the following example:

```
(define whatever
  (lambda (param)
    (if (< param 8)
        29
        (if (> param 2000)
            (* param 800)
            (+ 2  (/ param 4))))))
```

The second line is indented two spaces to indicate that it's enclosed within the form started on the previous line. The third and fourth are similarly indented. The fifth line is the *else-part* of an `if` form, so it is indented the same amount as the previous line to show that it belongs as part of the form enclosing the previous line. Similarly, the two parts of the second `if` form are indented two space from it.

Indentation is an important part of program organization. It helps you read the program and understand its parts. The program has a *shape* on the page that explains its structure.

Make sure, in this as in all future labs, that your code is thoroughly commented.

Good programmers avoid writing redundant code. Write only the code you need in order to solve the problem. In particular, it is possible to write `overweight?` either with or without an `if` form. The version without `if` is clearer and much better.

We have broken the problem down into "mind-size" pieces so that you can concentrate upon each task without having to keep the big picture in front of you all the time. This is the secret of good program design. As you write each procedure, ask yourself how you can use the procedures you have already written.

CHECKPOINT

1. What is the value of `(if (if (> 3 2) (< 4 5) (= 7 8)) #f #t)`?

2. Write an `if` form to compute the value of a collection of apples, where n is the number of apples. If there are more than 10 apples, the cost is 10*n*. If there are less than 4, the cost is 15*n*. Otherwise the cost is 12*n*.

3. In the Post Office problem, does the cost as a function of weight change smoothly or does it take any jumps?

DURING THE LAB

1. Using your text editor, enter your `weight-charge` procedure. Test it using the test data you wrote down earlier. Check that the results were as expected. Get a printout that shows the procedure works correctly.
2. Enter and test your distance factor procedure. Get a printout.
3. Enter and test `overweight?`. Get a printout.
4. Enter and test your volume factor procedure. Get a printout.
5. Enter and test your total cost procedure. Get a printout.

AFTER THE LAB

1. Write a brief report explaining how you went about selecting test data to ensure that the post office program works properly.
2. Joel User insists that his method of program testing is better than the method in this lab. Joel doesn't test any of the code when he enters it, but tests the whole program at once, and fixes bugs as necessary. Is he right? Why or why not? Is his method more or less likely to detect bugs that ours? Is his method likely to be faster than ours? Why or why not?

DELIVERABLES

1. A listing of your complete, final post-office program.
2. The printouts from each of your test runs for each procedure.
3. Your observations about the rules and definitions for procedures.

FOR FURTHER INVESTIGATION

The government gives scholarships to students depending upon their grade-point average (GPA), based upon a scale of 0 to 4. The amount of the scholarship is calculated according to the following rules:

- if the GPA is less than 2.5, nothing;
- if the GPA is less than 3.0, $100;
- if the GPA is less than 3.5, $200;
- otherwise, the amount is calculated by subtracting 3.0 from the GPA, and multiplying the result by $2000.

Each student takes five courses, whose marks are given as a percentage. the GPA is calculated by averaging the student's best four marks, and then dividing the result by 25. For example, suppose that John got 81% in English, 67% in chemistry, 72% in math, 89% in French, and 88% in physics. John's average mark is $(81 + 72 + 89 + 88)/4 = 82.5$, which translates to a GPA of 3.3.

Your job is to write a procedure which takes the five student grades as arguments, and outputs the amount of the scholarship. Your procedure will be used as follows:

```
(scholarship-amount 81 67 72 89 88)
```

Hint: Write two helper procedures: one will find the GPA corresponding to the average of four marks, and one will compute the scholarship amount from the GPA. Then the only messy part left is to identify which are the four grades to be used for the calculation.

Before you run the program, make some test cases that will test every possible case. How many cases are there that you must check? For each of your test cases, show the grade values and an explanation of what is being tested.

Deliverables: A listing of your code; a listing of your test cases; and a transcript showing that it works (i.e., that it produces the correct results for all of your test cases).

Lab 4
Financial Planning

In many problems, a computer model can be useful to help understand complex systems. In this lab we will use recursion to build a simple tax planning model. You will see that a single recursion pattern can be used to build many different recursive procedures, each of which computes a slightly different result.

WHAT YOU NEED TO KNOW

Make sure you have read up to the end of Section 2.2.

PROBLEM STATEMENT

Many countries, including Canada and the United States, provide tax relief to encourage people who save for their retirement. The details differ, but the basic idea is the same: deposits to a retirement savings account[1] are deducted from the taxpayer's income when tax is computed. When the taxpayer retires, the account is closed, at which point the entire balance is subject to taxation. (Most countries provide methods for deferring tax payments when a retirement account is closed.)

For example, a taxpayer might have $1000 per year (before taxes) that can be deposited into a retirement savings account. Assuming a tax rate of 30%, this leaves $700 for the actual deposit. Alternatively, the taxpayer can deposit the $1000 into a retirement account. In this case, the full amount is deposited, but when the account is closed, tax must be paid on the balance.

On the surface, it doesn't seem as though this method really benefits the taxpayer. Tax is either paid each year (in the savings scenario) or on retirement (in the retirement plan scenario). One important difference between the two scenarios is that tax *is* paid on each year's savings account interest, but no tax is paid on either deposits into a retirement account or interest paid until the account is closed.

In this lab, we want to see whether the total tax paid in the savings account scenario is more than, less than, or the same as that paid in the retirement plan scenario. To keep things simple, we will assume that the tax rate is constant (a so-called "flat tax"). This assumption is not true in Canada or the U.S.: the rate generally increases with increasing income (this is known as "progressive taxation"). We will also assume that no tax shelters (methods for legally avoiding having to pay tax) are available when the retirement account is closed.

We can write a procedure for each investment method to compute the final balance in the account, after all taxes have been deducted. The savings account procedure will have the following specification.

PROCEDURE (`savings-account` *amount tax-rate interest-rate years*)
ARGUMENTS
- *amount* is the dollar value being deposited each year
- *tax-rate* is the tax rate being charged on both income and interest, expressed as a decimal (not a percentage)
- *interest-rate* is the annual rate paid on the balance in the account, expressed as a decimal (not a percentage)
- *years* is the number of years the account is open
RETURNS   the total amount in the account after the specified number of years

---

[1] Known as a Registered Retirement Savings Plan in Canada, and an Investment Retirement Account in the U.S.

BEFORE THE LAB

1. Write the procedure for the savings account scenario. This procedure should accept an annual deposit amount, an interest rate, and a number of years, and should return the total amount on deposit at the end of that period, following the above specification. For example, we would evaluate

   ```
   (savings-account 1000 0.30 0.08 20)
   ```

   to compute the total balance on hand after 20 years, with an annual deposit of $700 after taxes, and an interest rate of 8%.

2. Evaluate

   ```
   (savings-account 1250 0.20 0.10 5)
   ```

   on paper, using the Droid Model.

PITFALLS AND ADVICE

1. Make sure you understand the problem. The savings account process consists of the following steps:
   - At the beginning of each year, the investor makes a deposit. This deposit is subject to taxation, and only the net amount after taxation is actually deposited.[2]
   - At the end of each year, interest is computed on the current balance. This interest is taxed, and only the net amount after taxation is deposited.

   Therefore, there are *two* tax charges per year: one for the deposit, and one for the interest.

2. Make sure that your recursive procedures each have a base case and a recursion case.

3. Make sure that you are correctly deducting income tax not only from the annual deposit, but also from the interest paid each year.

4. Convince yourself that helpers are extremely useful in solving this problem.

CHECKPOINT

Suppose we define

```
(define mystery
  (lambda (x y)
    (if (= x y)
        (+ x 3)
        (+ (* 2 x) (mystery (- x 1) y)))))
```

1. Evaluate (mystery 4 2) using the Droid model.
2. What is mystery's base case? What is mystery's recursion case?
3. There are values of x and y for which mystery can't compute a result. Find an example.

DURING THE LAB

1. Type in your solution into a file. Confirm that it works by evaluating

   ```
   (savings-account 1250 0.20 0.10 5)
   ```

   and checking the returned value against your hand-computed value. Produce a printout showing a trace of the procedure. To begin tracing a procedure, type (trace *procedure-name*). To stop tracing

---

[2] In the real world, tax is paid on income, not savings. This program doesn't attempt to model the actual payment of income tax; it is just a financial model. You can think of the user as saying "I have $1000 available to deposit, but I'll have to pay $300 on it. Therefore, I will deposit $700 in my account, and put the other $300 aside for my tax payment." To provide the same interface as the retirement procedure, our savings account procedure accepts the gross deposit as an argument, and computes the amount to put aside for tax.

a procedure, type (untrace *procedure-name*). The format of the trace output in your system might be slightly different from that of the book.

2. Using cut-and-paste, make a copy of your savings-account procedure (and its helper, if appropriate). Change the name of the copied procedure to retirement-account, and change the helper's name similarly. Modify the procedure and its helper so that it does not deduct tax on deposits or interest, but only on the total balance at the end when the account is closed. Produce a trace of the evaluation of

```
(retirement-account 1250 0.20 0.10 5)
```

3. Finally, write a procedure that accepts the same arguments as savings-account and retirement-account. It should call each of these procedures with these arguments, and compute the difference in tax paid between the two scenarios. Test your final program by calling this procedure to find the difference between the two methods when the tax rate is 30%, the annual deposit is $2000, the interest rate is 9%, and the account is open for 10 years. Produce a printout showing a trace of both procedures.

AFTER THE LAB

1. What are the tax benefits (if any) of a retirement savings account, according to our model?
2. We insisted you use helpers. Try to write savings-account without using a helper. Can you do it? Is it more or less clear than the version with a helper? Why or why not?
3. Write retirement-account without using a helper. Which version do you prefer? Why?

DELIVERABLES

1. your "Before The Lab" work
2. a fully-commented listing of your procedures
3. the traces from "During The Lab"
4. your "After The Lab" work

Lab 5
Recursion and Rabbits

OBJECTIVES

Recursion allows you to write, in just a few lines, a program that does enormous amounts of computation. As we saw in Section 2.3, there are better and worse ways of doing a computation. This lab will give you some practice in designing recursive procedures and analyzing their complexity.

WHAT YOU NEED TO KNOW

Read up to the end of Section 2.3. Make sure you understand complexity and recursive procedures.

PROBLEM STATEMENT

The 13th century mathematician Leonardo of Pisa (also known as Leonardo Fibonacci, and not the same person as Leonardo da Vinci) was interested in how rabbits breed. He devised a mathematical model of the number of rabbits in successive generations. The numbers his model produces are known as the *Fibonacci numbers*, and are computed according to the following rule, where $F(n)$ is the nth Fibonacci number:

$$F(n) = F(n-1) + F(n-2) \qquad (n > 1)$$

$$F(n) = 1 \qquad (n \leq 1)$$

The Fibonacci numbers are: 1, 1, 2, 3, 5, 8, 13, ... They have many applications in mathematics and computer science (apart from modeling rabbit procreation). One advanced algorithm for sorting data (polyphase merge) organizes the data in groups whose sizes are Fibonacci numbers. Fibonacci numbers occur in many problems in computer science and mathematics; it is ironic that they don't actually do a good job of counting rabbits.

Joel User has written a Scheme procedure to calculate $F(n)$, as follows:

```
;;; fib: compute Fibonacci numbers, by Joel User.
;;; This procedure accepts a positive number, n,
;;; and computes F(n) according to the relationship
;;;     F(n) = F(n-1) + F(n-2)       n > 1
;;;     F(n) = 1                      n <= 1
(define fib
  (lambda (n)
    (if (<= n 1)
      1
      (+ (fib (- n 1)) (fib (- n 2))))))
```

Joel's `fib` procedure is well-written. Notice the comments that explain the way in which the procedure works. It's well-indented; the name n is appropriate as a parameter name here, because that's the name used in the mathematical problem statement. `fib` also happens to give the correct answer in all cases.

Unfortunately, it is too slow to be usable, as this lab will convince you.

Before the Lab

1. Evaluate (fib 4), using the Droid Model. Take a rest! You probably had to work pretty hard to get the answer.

2. It's possible to rewrite fib to improve it, The new procedure will accept as arguments $F(n-1)$ and $F(n-2)$. You will write a helper procedure that starts like this

   ```
   (define fast-fib-helper
     (lambda (n curr-fib prev-fib)
       ...
   ```

   To compute $F(4)$, we call (fast-fib-helper 4 1 1):

   ```
   > (trace fast-fib-helper)
   > (fast-fib-helper 4 1 1)
   call fast-fib-helper: 4 1 1
   | call fast-fib-helper: 3 2 1
   | | call fast-fib-helper: 2 3 2
   | | | call fast-fib-helper: 1 5 3
   | | | return from fast-fib-helper: 5
   | | return from fast-fib-helper: 5
   | return from fast-fib-helper: 5
   return from fast-fib-helper: 5
   5
   ```

   fast-fib-helper's last two arguments are the current and previous Fibonacci numbers. fast-fib-helper is not intended to be called by the user. It will have a calling procedure that has the same interface as does fib. The caller's n argument is the goal, the number of the Fibonacci number to be computed. fast-fib-helper's n argument is a counter that tells how much of the computation has been done; when fast-fib-helper is called with n equal to 0, the process is complete.

3. Study the trace carefully. What is the termination condition for fast-fib-helper? Which parameter contains the result when fast-fib-helper terminates?

4. Assume that fast-fib-helper is to be tail-recursive. Answer each of these questions with an algebraic formula. How should the new-fib argument be computed in the recursive call? How should the curr-fib argument of the recursive call be computed? How should the prev-fib argument of the recursive call be computed? Again, studying the trace will help you answer this question.

5. Write fast-fib-helper.

Pitfalls and Advice

What is the recursion variable?

Checkpoint

1. What does the Scheme primitive trace do?
2. The recursive procedure

   ```
   (define foo
     (lambda (n)
       (if (= n 0)
           1
           (* (+ n 2)
              (* (bar n) (foo (sub1 n)))))))
   ```

   calls bar. Each time bar is called it performs n multiplications. How many multiplications are performed when (foo n) is evaluated, in big-oh notation?
3. Will (fib 2.5) terminate or will it run forever?

DURING THE LAB

1. One way we can investigate why is by tracing the procedure. Type Joel's `fib` procedure into Scheme, trace it, and run it with different values of n.

2. Evaluate `(fib 6)`. Get a printout of your trace, and study it carefully. *Don't print out the trace of anything bigger than* `(fib 6)`—*it's a waste of paper*,

3. Turn off tracing, and evaluate `(fib 25)`. Your machine might pause for a while. Using your watch or a clock, find out how much time is taken.[1] (Some Scheme systems provide a feature to tell you how long it takes to evaluate a form. If your system has such a feature, use it.) Find out how long it takes to evaluate `(fib 24)`, `(fib 23)`,..., `(fib 20)`. (If you are using a very fast computer and Scheme system, these times might be very short. In this case, use larger values of *n*.

4. Enter your new improved `fast-fib-helper` procedure and demonstrate that your revised procedure computes the correct answer.

5. Trace `fast-fib-helper`, and get a printout of the evaluation of `(fast-fib-helper 6 1 1)`.

6. Turn off tracing, and find the times needed by `fast-fib-helper` to compute the same Fibonacci numbers you computed with `fib`.

AFTER THE LAB

1. Examine your time figures, and derive a formula that tells you how much more time `(fib (add1 n))` will take to evaluate than `(fib n)` takes. (There are many factors that can contribute to execution time, so don't expect your formula to be dead-on.)

2. Do the same for `fast-fib-helper`.

3. Examine the trace output for the two procedures, and derive a "big-oh" formula for the time complexity of each procedure. (Hint: assume that `(fib n)` takes *k* calls to evaluate. How many more calls will `(fib (add1 n))` take?) Is there a significant difference between the time complexity of `fib` and `fast-fib` for large n?

4. How well do the big-oh formulas match the time formulas?

5. Is there some advice you would give to Joel[2] about writing programs? In all the computing that `fib` does, what operations could be avoided (and are avoided in `fib`). The answer is not "use a tail-recursive procedure"!

6. In the lab, we wrote `fast-fib-helper` to use a counter that goes from *n* down to 0. Write a version of `fast-fib-helper` that counts from 0 up to *n*. Which version is better? Why?

DELIVERABLES

1. trace runs for the two Fibonacci procedures, along with a printout of your Fibonacci procedure

2. your formulas (and accompanying work) that compare the two versions, from "After the Lab"

3. your advice to Joel, from "After the Lab"

---

[1] On a 66MHz 486DX2 running the scm system it took nearly 20 seconds.

[2] It would appear from his frequent fumbles throughout the book that he isn't likely to take anybody's advice.

Cryptographic Operators

Codemakers have for centuries devised cipher and code systems that are partly fixed and partly variable. Many machines were built to encrypt according to these systems. With machines, the variable part might be a key (a string of numbers and letters) or a small box that plugs into the encryption machine.

In this lab, you will experiment with encryption and decryption procedures that are designed in a similar way, accepting procedural arguments that correspond to the variable parts of the encryption system.

WHAT YOU NEED TO KNOW

Read Chapter 3 up through Section 3.3.

PROBLEM STATEMENT

A cipher is a method of encrypting text by replacing individual characters. As we discovered in Section 3.1, a code replaces words in a text. Decrypting the text after ciphering means "undoing" the transformation character by character. For a code, each word must be handled separately.

We can also alter the text (a string) by reordering it, by rearranging the position of the characters in the string.

We are going to build a set of cryptographic procedures that include ciphers as well as procedures that reorder strings. We'll also build procedures that create cryptographic procedures whose action depends on the input to the procedure that creates them.

Ciphers

The first kind of cryptographic procedure we want is an *encrypter*, a procedure that transforms a character into a new character under some ciphering scheme. The scheme can either be a numerical calculation, like the Caesar cipher, or it can be specified by a table, as we will do here. For convenience, the result of an encrypter is a string with just that one new character. The goodie `crypt.scm` contains the `caesar-encrypt-char` procedure from the text. Its input is a character and it returns a string one character long.

A *table-encrypter* procedure takes an alphabetic character and returns a string of one new character, according to a transformation specified by a table: the character is transformed into `letter->number` (from Chapter 3), then used to index into a *cipher-table*, a string of 26 lower-case alphabetic characters in which no character appears more than once.

```
(define a-table-encrypter
  (lambda (c)
    (string
      (string-ref
        "zyxwvutsrqponmlkjihgfedcba"
        (letter->number c)))))
```

To generalize the idea of a table-encrypter, we can write a procedure `make-table-encrypt` that takes a cipher-table and returns a table-encrypter procedure using that string.

PROCEDURE (make-table-encrypt *cipher-table*)

ARGUMENTS

- *cipher-table* is a string of 26 lower-case alphabetic characters in which no character appears more than once

RETURNS   a table-encrypter procedure

Reordering strings

"Shuffling" two strings is creating a new string in which the characters at consecutive even positions are taken from the first string and characters at consecutive odd positions are taken from the second string.

```
> (shuffle "abcde" "fghij")
"afbgchdiej"
```

PROCEDURE (shuffle *s1 s2*)

ARGUMENTS

- *s1* is a string
- *s2* is a string of the same length as *s1*

RETURNS   a new string in which the character at position $2i$ comes from position i in *s1*, and the character at position $2i + 1$ comes from position i in *s2*.

---

unshuffle is a corresponding procedure that reverses the shuffling procedure:

PROCEDURE (unshuffle *s*)

ARGUMENTS

- *s* is a string of even length

RETURNS   a pair of strings s1 and s2 such that (shuffle s1 s2) is *s*

```
> (unshuffle "afbgchdiej")
( "abcde" . "fghij")
```

The procedure (zap s) splits a string in two (you will probably want to write split) and then shuffles the result. Assume s has even length.

```
> (zap "afbgchdiej")
"ahfdbigecj"
```

PROCEDURE (split *s*)

ARGUMENTS

- *s* is a string

RETURNS   a pair of strings s1 and s2 in which s1 contains the first half of *s* and s2 the second half of *s*.

PROCEDURE (zap *s*)

ARGUMENTS

- *s* is a string

RETURNS   a new string in which the first half and second half of *s* are shuffled.

The procedure (unzap s) undoes the operation of zap, so that:

```
> (unzap (zap "abcdefgh"))
"abcdefgh"
```

PROCEDURE (unzap *s*)

ARGUMENTS

- *s* is a string

RETURNS   a new string such that (unzap (zap s)) is *s*

Creating cryptographic procedures

encrypt-string takes an encrypter procedure and returns a procedure that applies that procedure to a string.

PROCEDURE (encrypt-string *cproc*)

ARGUMENTS

- *cproc* is an encrypter procedure

RETURNS   a procedure that applies *cproc* to a string

---

encrypt-twice takes two string cryptographic procedures and returns a procedure that applies the first, then the second procedure to a string.

```
> (define caes-encrypt (encrypt-string caesar-encrypt-char))
> (caes-encrypt "help")
"khos"
> (define zap-caes (encrypt-twice zap caes-encrypt))
> (zap-caes "help")
"kohs"
```

PROCEDURE (encrypt-twice *sproc1 sproc2*)

ARGUMENTS

- *sproc1* is a string procedure that encrypts a string
- *sproc2* is a string procedure that encrypts a string

RETURNS   a procedure that applies *sproc1* to a string and then *sproc2*

---

caesar-decrypt-char undoes the effects of the Caesar cipher. We will need to devise a composition of two decryption procedures to undo the effects of zap-caes. We can use encrypt-twice to do this.

BEFORE THE LAB

1. Design make-table-encrypt and appropriate tests for it.
2. Design shuffle and unshuffle, and their tests.
3. Design zap, unzap, and split and their tests.
4. Design encrypt-string and encrypt-twice and tests to show they work.

PITFALLS AND ADVICE

It is easy to confuse a string with one character with a character. Don't.

CHECKPOINT

1. What does the procedure string return? What is the difference between string and string??
2. Describe a way to handle character sets where the alphabetic characters are not in order, in implementing a "table-enencrypt-twice" procedure.
3. What is the value of (zap "0123456789")?

During the Lab

Load the goodie `crypt`.

1. Enter `make-table-encrypt` and test it with a variety of inputs.
2. Type in `shuffle` and `unshuffle`. It may be helpful to write a procedure that shuffles two strings and unshuffles them and compares the results to the input, for testing.
3. Type in `zap`, `unzap`, and `split` and test them.
4. Enter `encrypt-string` and `encrypt-twice` and test them.

After the Lab

1. What is the essential property of all the encryption and ciphering procedures that allows us to undo their effects? (Hint: What if there were repeated characters in the cipher-table in a table-encrypter procedure?)
2. Are there any encryption procedures that we couldn't undo?

Deliverables

1. listings of your procedures: `make-table-encrypt`, `shuffle`, `unshuffle`, `zap`, `unzap`, `split`, `encrypt-string`, and `encrypt-twice`.
2. a transcript or transcripts showing testing for these procedures
3. your answer to the "After the Lab" questions

For Further Investigation

Another useful cryptographic process is to insert a character of the real text into the encrypted string after k characters from a meaningless "carrier" string. We will provide give you a meaningless string to be used as carrier. Use it and when it runs out start again at its beginning.

Write a procedure `insert-message`:

```
> (insert-message "yes" "zxqvb" 2)
"zxyqvebzs"
```

PROCEDURE (`insert-message` *message carrier k*)

ARGUMENTS
- *message* is a message string
- *carrier* is a meaningless carrier string
- k is the number of carrier characters to insert

RETURNS   a new string composed of k carrier characters followed by a character from *message*, repeated until the entire *message* is encoded

---

The inverse procedure `extract-message` creates a message string from an encoded message:

PROCEDURE (`extract-message` *encoded k*)

ARGUMENTS
- *encoded* is an encoded message string
- k is the number of carrier characters to skip

RETURNS   a new string got by skipping k carrier characters then extracting the real character until the *encoded* is all used up

---

Deliverables: a listing of `insert-message` and `extract-message` and a transcript showing that they work.

Lab 7

An Interactive Lunar Lander

OBJECTIVES

This lab demonstrates how to build interactive programs. It helps you with graphics, recursive procedure, interaction, and strings.

Our first lunar lander program in Chapter 2 simulates *n* seconds of flight with only initial settings, and no output except the final result, a numeric code. In this lab you will improve its output from numbers to strings, change the program to accept input as it runs, and finally build a simple graphical display of its progress.

WHAT YOU NEED TO KNOW

Read Chapter 3 up through Section 3.4. Make sure you understand formatted output, strings, and Scheme's graphics primitives.

PROBLEM STATEMENT

In Chapter 2 we implemented a Lunar Lander game, lander, a program for landing a lunar exploration vehicle on the moon. lander is a recursive procedure that we supply an initial velocity, height, and fuel, as well as the fuel-rate and the duration of the rocket firing. If we're correct, the lander arrives at height 0 with velocity in a range of safe landing velocities.

We've cleaned up the version of lander that appears in the text, giving us new-lander, which has the same interface. The code for the old and new lander programs appears in the goodie land.scm. A description of the interface to the procedure new-lander follows; the implementation is shown in Program 7-1.

PROCEDURE (new-lander *vel height fuel fuel-rate seconds*)

ARGUMENTS
- *vel* is the initial velocity
- *height* is the distance above the ground
- *fuel* is the total fuel
- *fuel-rate* is the fuel burn rate
- *seconds* is the duration of the burn

RETURNS   a code indicating whether the vehicle has crashed (0), landed (1), escaped (2), run out of time (3), or out of fuel (-1)

In order to make an interactive Lander program based on new-lander, we should first replace the clumsy numerical result codes. The result codes of new-lander are:
- time over 3
- safe landing 1
- escape 2
- crash 0
- out of fuel -1

We would prefer a procedure that produces descriptive strings instead. In each of the following messages, *xxx* are replaced by the corresponding values.

```
(define check-velocity
  (lambda (vel)
    (if (< vel escape) 2
      (if (< vel max-safe-velocity) 1 0))))
(define new-lander
  (lambda (vel height fuel fuel-rate seconds)
    (if (<= height 0)
      (check-velocity vel)
      (if (= seconds 0)
        3
        (if (<= fuel 0)
          -1
          (if (< vel escape)
            2
            (new-lander
              (- (+ vel gravity) (/ (min fuel fuel-rate) mass))
                  (- height vel)
                  (- fuel fuel-rate)
                  fuel-rate
                  (sub1 seconds)))))))))
```

Program 7-1   Lander

- Height *xxx*, velocity *xxx*, t=0
- Safe landing, velocity *xxx*
- Escaped from the moon, height *xxx* velocity *xxx*
- Crashed, velocity *xxx*
- Height *xxx*, velocity *xxx*, no fuel

We'll call our new version string-lander. We'll need to rewrite check-velocity and new-lander to produce these messages, using the real values of height and velocity. These procedures will print the message at the conclusion of each run of the game.

string-lander still only takes the input for a burn and returns a final result. An interactive lander procedurewould, at the end of each burn, display the velocity and height of the lander and the remaining fuel, and ask you for new fuel-rate settings and the length of the burn. How interactive-lander would act is shown in Figure 7-1.

```
> (interactive-lander 10 100 100000 2000 1)
Velocity: 10.04 Height: 90 Fuel: 98000
Enter fuel rate and number of seconds: 2000 3
Velocity: 10.159999999999997 Height: 59.76000000000001 Fuel: 92000
Enter fuel rate and number of seconds: 3000 3
Velocity: 7.279999999999994 Height: 32.160000000000025 Fuel: 83000
Enter fuel rate and number of seconds: 2000 2
Velocity: 7.359999999999992 Height: 17.560000000000038 Fuel: 79000
Enter fuel rate and number of seconds: 3000 1
Velocity: 6.3999999999999915 Height: 10.200000000000045 Fuel: 76000
Enter fuel rate and number of seconds: 3000 1
Velocity: 5.439999999999991 Height: 3.800000000000054 Fuel: 73000
Enter fuel rate and number of seconds: 4000 1
"Safe landing, velocity 3.4799999999999907"
```

Figure 7-1   Output of interactive lander

The structure of interactive-lander is not necessarily the same as new-lander. Before asking the user for input, you might test whether the vehicle has landed, run out of fuel, or escaped from the moon's gravity.

The final product will be graphical-lander, a version of interactive-lander that displays the movement of the lander on a graphics window. The interaction should be the same, but the position of the lander on the window should be updated on a graphic window every second. Every refresh seconds the window should be cleared and the lander drawn on a clear screen.

We will need to call a procedure to begin the graphics, and then run the main lander simulation with graphics. We'll call this procedure start-graphical-lander. It can have an internal helper that does the simulation. A description of the interface to the procedure start-graphical-lander follows.

PROCEDURE (start-graphical-lander *vel height fuel fuel-rate seconds refresh*)

ARGUMENTS
- *vel* is the initial velocity
- *height* is the distance above the ground
- *fuel* is the total fuel
- *fuel-rate* is the fuel burn rate
- *seconds* is the duration of the burn
- *refresh* is the number of seconds before the window is cleared and redrawn

EFFECT   draws a graphic simulation of the lander and displays a message at the game's end describing what has happened to the vehicle

---

(start-graphical-lander 10 100 100000 2000 1 5) starts the interaction, and sets the refresh to be every 5 seconds.

BEFORE THE LAB

1. Sketch out an interaction between the user and the computer while playing the game. What commands does the user type in? What are the computer responses?
2. Design your version of the procedures.
3. Create a set of test inputs that should test your program.

PITFALLS AND ADVICE

Make sure you understand the difference between displaying a string and returning it as the value of a procedure.

CHECKPOINT

1. Write a format form that will produce the string Height 2000, velocity 100, no fuel when height and velocity have the values 2000 and 100.
2. What Scheme form do you use to evaluate a sequence of forms in order?
3. In graphical-lander, what graphics form must be evaluated every refresh seconds?

DURING THE LAB

1. Type in string-lander and your new version of check-velocity. Test them out to show that all results are properly reported.
2. Implement interactive-lander and demonstrate that it works.
3. Enter your graphical lander procedures, test that they work, and get a plot of the graphical output of the game.

AFTER THE LAB

1. How could you make the game better? There are two aspects to such a game: realistic behavior of the simulated world, and interesting interaction (control) of the objects.

2. There are some simplifications in the lander. Can you identify any? How would you improve the simulation?

3. Are there better ways to control the lander? We could use the characters "u" and "d" to alter the fuel rate. Outline how that would affect the design of `interactive-lander`.

DELIVERABLES

1. listings of the procedures you have written and the testing output
2. a plot showing the graphical output of `graphical-lander`
3. answers to the "After the lab" questions

FOR FURTHER INVESTIGATION

Enhance the graphical lander to make it more realistic. This might involve adding scenery such as boulders, craters, crevasses, and the like, as shown in Figure 7-2. You might also make the lander's behavior more realistic, by accounting for the fuel rate and other factors (this will require some physics). A sophisticated lander would allow a horizontal velocity, accomplished by small jets at the sides; the lander in the figure appears to be in trouble if it can't move sideways.

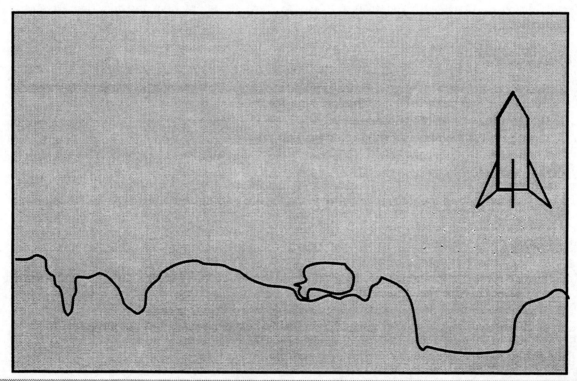

Figure 7-2   A sophisticated graphical lander

If you want to get really adventurous, you can modify the lander program so that it knows whether the landing was safe. We can define a safe landing as one where the ground is flat. In Chapter 4, you will learn how the heights of the ground at various places can be kept in a list. For now, you can write a procedure that gives the actual height of the ground for a given x coordinate, using a giant if form.

```
(define ground-height
  (lambda (x)
    (if (< x 20)
      10.5
      (if (< x 27)
        6.2
        ...))))
```

You can then require that the ground underneath the lander be flat, i.e., that the height on one side is roughly equal to the height on the other.

Deliverables: Your program listing and a demonstration (it's hard to print out the execution of a graphical program).

Defining a New Data Type

OBJECTIVES

Abstract data types let us divide problems into two parts: finding a representation (the implementation of the ADT) and using the representation in the solution to the problem.

This lab presents an example problem on the time of day that lets us learn about representing a numeric value composed of several parts, and input in several forms. We will describe its ADT, implement it, and build procedures to display its value and read a string representing the time of day.

WHAT YOU NEED TO KNOW

Read Chapter 3 up through Section 3.4. Make sure you understand strings, ADTs, and the location example in Section 3.4.3.

PROBLEM STATEMENT

Suppose we are writing a program to control a microwave oven. The program would have to keep several time values, such as the start time and duration. We have seen several data types that are built into Scheme. The daytime data type isn't built in, but that doesn't stop us from defining an Abstract Data Type for representing the time of day, shown in Figure 8-1. Figure 8-2 gives some examples of this ADT.

```
> (define breakfast (make-time-12 7 30 00 #\a))
> (define dinner (make-time-12 6 30 00 #\p))
> (define lunch (make-time-12 12 01 00 #\p))
> (time-hours-12 breakfast) ⇒ -7
> (time-minutes breakfast) ⇒ 30
> (time-seconds breakfast) ⇒ 0
> (time-hours-12 dinner) ⇒ 6
> (time-minutes dinner) ⇒ 30
> (time-seconds dinner) ⇒ 0
> (time-hours-12 lunch) ⇒ 12
> (time-minutes lunch) ⇒ 0
> (time-hours-24 lunch) ⇒ 12
> (time-hours-24 breakfast) ⇒ 7
> (time-hours-24 dinner) ⇒ 18
```

Figure 8-2   Using the daytime ADT

The daytime ADT would be useful in many other applications besides microwave ovens. We could use it in digital clocks and alarm systems, as well.

We will need to specify an ADT for time of day. For convenience, we would like to create time of day both on a 12 and 24 hour clock (like that used in airlines and railways). We will need to specify a.m. or p.m. for the 12 hour times. Although there are constructors for both 12 and 24 hour times, they both use make-time, an "internal" constructor.

We also need a procedure to display the time as a string: time->12string prints the time of day according to the 12 hour clock and time->24string prints the time of day according to the 24 hour clock. The output

Constructors

- (make-time-24 *hour minutes seconds*)
  Return a daytime with the specified components.
- (make-time-12 *hour minutes seconds am/pm*)
  Return a daytime interpreted as twelve hour times, with the specified components. *am/pm* is the character #*a* for morning and #*p* for afternoon.
- (string->time *time-string*)
  Return a daytime whose external representation is *time-string*. [handwritten: string → number of seconds i.e. 12 + 30 + 23]

Accessors

- (time-hours-12 *daytime*)
  Return the hours of *daytime*, in the twelve-hour clock system. We represent this value as a number which is negative for am, and positive for pm.
- (time-hours-24 *daytime*)
  Return the hours of *daytime*, in the twenty-four clock system.
- (time-minutes *daytime*)
  Return the minutes of *daytime*.
- (time-seconds *daytime*)
  Return the seconds of *daytime*.

Output procedures

- (time->24string *daytime*)
  Print *daytime* in twenty-hour format.
- (time->12string *daytime*)
  Print *daytime* in twelve-hour format.

Figure 8-1   Abstract Data Type: daytime

should be in the form HH:MM:SS for the 24 hour clock, where the hour ranges from 00 to 23. In the 24 hour clock the hour always has two digits.

For the 12 hour clock the output format should be HH:MM:SS AP. AP is either am or pm, for example 09:10:11 am.

In order to construct the output string, you'll need to take the number in question and create a two-character string (for minutes and seconds) that represents it. The text states that the first argument to format must be #t, in which case the string is printed. If the first argument is #f, however, Scheme just returns the string representing the output. The basic format does not accept any information in the format string to describe the number of characters to print a number. Thus (format #f "˜a" 7) ⇒ "7". To get a two-character string, you must append the string "0" to its front.

It would be most convenient also to read a time of day as a string and create a string that represents the time of day:

```
> (define breakfast (string->time "7:30:00 am"))
> (time-minutes breakfast)
30
> (time->12string breakfast)
"7:30:00 am"
```

To implement this you'll have to build a procedure to convert two consecutive characters into a number.

BEFORE THE LAB

1. Write a module to implement the ADT, except for the string input and output procedures.
2. Design a test driver procedure that determine whether your code properly implements the ADT. Write down on paper the output your test driver produces.
3. Design the code to implement the string conversion procedures. Use your ADT constructors to implement them. Design the output procedure.

4. Design the input procedure. This is harder.
5. Write a procedure that gives the number of seconds between two times. Assume that the first time is no later than the second.

PITFALLS AND ADVICE

Watch out for "007:3:0 am"—it's legal. Make sure your input and output formats are consistent.

CHECKPOINT

1. Show the internal representations of (make-time 24 13 1 2) and (make-time-12 3 4 5 #\p).
2. How can you compute the number corresponding to a character between #\0 and #\9?
3. Write a Scheme form that returns a two-character string representing any number between 1 and 99.

DURING THE LAB

1. Type in your implementation of the daytime ADT and the test driver.
2. Test the make-time- constructors and the accessors.
3. Next test the output procedures: the 24 hour procedure should be simpler, so start with it.
4. Test the string input procedures, starting with the 24 hour input, and then doing the 12 hour input.
5. Implement the procedure that gives the number of seconds between two times, and show that it works.

AFTER THE LAB

We could use a similar implementation to represent the day of the year. Briefly sketch out its ADT and an implementation.

DELIVERABLES

1. a listing of your implementation of the daytime ADT and the test driver for testing the implementation
2. a transcript showing that your code properly implements the ADT, including the several different constructors, the accessors, the two different output procedures and the string input procedures
3. a listing of the procedure that gives the number of seconds between two times, and a printout showing that it works
4. the answer to the "After the Lab" question

FOR FURTHER INVESTIGATION

We would like to build a program to create a string representing a real number. Since the computer has only a finite number of bits to represent the number, the string to represent a number has only a finite number of characters. In fact the Scheme primitive (number->string num) will produce the string corresponding to a number.

We usually ask a program to print floating point numbers with only a few digits to the right of the decimal point. To simplify things, we'll focus on the problem of creating a string that represents numbers greater than 0 and less than 1. We'll write a procedure to print a floating-point number in that range to d digits. The last digit should be rounded. We'll call the procedure print-float.

How can we implement it? Here's a strategy: if we multiply the positive number (and less than 1) by the appropriate power of 10, we have a floating-point number that can be converted to an integer and then printed. Look back at the sidebar "Numbers in Scheme" in Chapter 2 to find out how to round a number (convert it to the nearest integer) and how to convert that number to an exact number (one with no numbers, even 0, after the decimal point).

Once you have a rounded, exact number, it's time to print. (`format #f "~a"`) will produce a number. But there's a problem. The number many not be *d* digits wide. Why? If it is not, add initial zeroes, using `string-append` to get a string of the desired width.

Deliverables: a listing of `print-float` and a printout showing how it works

Lab 9
Integration

OBJECTIVES

This lab provides experience in recursive procedures, gets you to embed a recursive procedure and deepens your understanding of procedures as arguments.

WHAT YOU NEED TO KNOW

1. Read the text through Chapter 3. You should understand how real numbers work in Scheme.
2. Review the plot procedures.

PROBLEM STATEMENT

In this lab, we need to find the area underneath a function f, called the *integral* of the function. The area is a region between the graph of the function and the x axis, over some range $x0$ to $x1$. We connect the x axis to the graph of the function at $x0$ and $x1$. We will do this numerically, although for many functions we can write down another function that directly expresses the area.

To compute the area numerically, we need to break up the interval $x0$ to $x1$ into n subintervals, and compute the area in each subinterval by some simple rule. The width of each subinterval, h, is $(x1 - x0)/n$. What will we use as its height? A simple rule is to use the average value of f over the interval. But actually approximating the average value would require knowing the value of f at all points. We can't do that numerically. Instead we use a simple approximation, the average of the values of f at the left, l, and right, r, endpoints of the subinterval. Then we can compute the area of the rectangle with that height and width h. Interestingly, this is the area of a trapezoid with height h and two sides $f(r)$ and $f(l)$. This way of approximating the integral is called the *trapezoidal* rule. Figure 9-1 shows the trapezoids (in dotted lines) fitting the curve $y = e^x$ over the range 0 to 4.

We will write a procedure (integrate-trap f x0 x1 n) that approximates the area of f from x0 to x1 using n subintervals:

PROCEDURE (integrate-trap f $x0$ $x1$ n)

ARGUMENTS
- f is a procedure of one numerical argument that returns a number
- $x0$ is a number that specifies the left end of the range
- $x1$ is a number that specifies the right end of the range
- n is the number of subintervals

RETURNS   the approximate area of f from $x0$ to $x1$

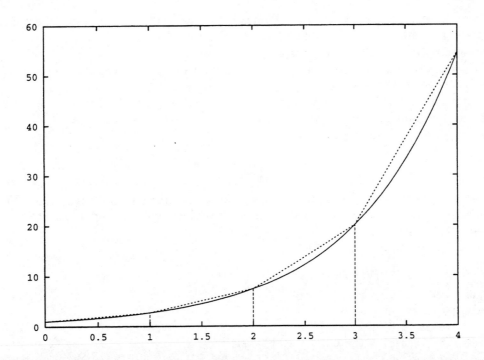

Figure 9-1   The trapezoid rule for e^x between 0 and 4, at spacing 1

It's easiest to start by writing a helper, `integrate-trap-h`.

PROCEDURE (`integrate-trap-h` f $x0$ h n)

ARGUMENTS

- f is a procedure of one numerical argument that returns a number
- $x0$ is a number that specifies the left end of the range
- h is the width of a subinterval
- n is the number of subintervals remaining

RETURNS   the approximate area of f from $x0$ using n intervals of width h

We will next embed `integrate-trap-h` in `integrate-h`. The two procedures share variables, so the helper can be simplified. Call this new procedure `new-integrate-trap`. Plan to do this in two steps. First embed the helper, using as a model the way we embedded `fact-helper` in `fact`. Don't forget to use `letrec`, since `integrate-trap-h` is a recursive procedure.

Get it working. How will you know whether it works? Next, remove shared variables.

The goodie `grate.scm` contains the following procedure:

```
(define make-quad
  (lambda (a b c)
    (lambda (x)
      (+ c
         (* x
            (+ b (* x a)))))))
```

(`make-quad a b c`) returns a procedure to evaluate the function $ax^2 + bx + c$, given x. You will use this procedure to create a quadratic function and numerically integrate it.

BEFORE THE LAB

1. Integrate x^2 by hand over the region 0 to 4. Draw the rectangles that you get using the trapezoid rule for intervals of width 1. Calculate the integral.
2. Write `integrate-trap` and `integrate-trap-h`.
3. Create a new procedure which is the result of embedding `integrate-trap-h` in `integrat-trap`. Call this procedure `new-integrate-trap`.
4. Remove the shared variables in `new-integrate-trap`, renaming it to `embed-integrate-trap`.
5. Write a new procedure (`inttrap n`) that computes (`integrate-trap q111 0 10 n`).
6. Write `inttrap2` that computes (`integrate-trap q111 10 100 n`).

CHECKPOINT

1. One way to loop over the n subintervals in `integrate-trap` is the take the range from x0 to x1, and starting with x0, add h until it reaches x1. What's the problem with this approach? (Notice that we didn't do it that way!)
2. Joel has written the following procedure:

```
(define joel
  (lambda (x y)
    (letrec
      ((help
        (lambda (a b c)
          (if (> a b) a (help (* c a) b)))))
    (help x y 2)))
```

Are there any shared variables that can be removed, to simplify the helper?
3. If you add (`/ 1.0 i`) to itself *i* times on a computer, does it add up to *exactly* 1.0 for all integers *i*? What does the answer to this question tell you about the programming you'll need to do in this lab?

DURING THE LAB

During the lab you will test the integration procedures you have written and then plot the results of `new-integrate-trap` over some ranges, varying the number of subintervals.

1. Load the goodie `grate.scm`.
2. Type in `integrate-trap` and `integrate-trap-h`. Define:

   (`define q111 (make-quad 1 1 1)`)

   Test `integrate-trap` over the range 0 to 10, using $n = 100$. Differential calculus tell us that the integral of a quadratic function over the range x0 to x1 is $a/3x_1^3 + b/2x_1^2 + cx_1 - a/3x_0^3 + b/2x_0^2 + cx_0$. To check your integration results, use the procedure (`int-q a b c x0 x1`), which evaluates the integral of $ax^2 + bx + c$ over the range x0 to x1. int-q is in the goodie.
   Compare the result of `integrate-trap` with (`int-q 1 1 1 0 10`).
3. Type in `new-integrate-trap` and test it.
4. Type in `embed-integrate-trap` and test it.
5. Using `inttrap`, compute (`integrate-trap q111 0 10 n`), for the values of n: 10, 100, 500, 1000, and 5000.
6. Plot by hand the results of `inttrap`.
7. Do the same process for q111 for the range 10 to 100, using `inttrap2`, for the same values of n. Plot the results by hand.

AFTER THE LAB

1. Explain how you embedded `integrate-trap-h` in `integrate-trap`. Explain how you simplified the resulting procedure.
2. Write down any observations you might have on how the result of the approximation improves or worsens as n changes.

DELIVERABLES

1. your hand-drawn plot of the rectangles for x^2 and your calculation for the integral
2. a listing of your `integrate-trap` and `integrate-trap-h`, and the test results and comparison with `int-q`
3. a listing of `new-integrate-trap` and `embed-integrate-trap` and printouts showing that they work
4. a listing of the values of `integrate-trap` as n varies
5. plots of the value `inttrap1` and `inttrap2`, and a listing of the results, as n varies from 10 to 100 to 500 to 1000 to 5000
6. your answers to the "After the Lab" questions

FOR FURTHER INVESTIGATION

The trapezoid rule essentially draws a line between successive points of the function. A quadratic (2nd order) curve connecting three points is generally a better approximation. A formula called Simpson's rule describes how to compute the value of the area under a quadratic approximation to three evenly spaced points, a, b, and c, separated by h. It is:

$$h/3 \times (f(a) + 4f(b) + f(c))$$

We calculate $h = (x1 - x0)/n$, and then apply Simpson's rule at $n/2$ intervals. In each interval, we compute f at x_l, the left endpoint of the subinterval, $x_l + h$, the midpoint, and $x_l + 2h$, the right endpoint.

PROCEDURE (`integrate-simp` f $x0$ $x1$ n)

ARGUMENTS
- f is a procedure of one numerical argument that returns a number
- $x0$ is a number that specifies the left end of the range
- $x1$ is a number that specifies the right end of the range
- n is the number of subintervals

RETURNS   the approximate area of f from $x0$ to $x1$

Instead of computing the approximation over fixed intervals, we can derive the integral by calculating the value of the function at a randomly chosen set of points. To understand how Scheme primitives can generate random numbers, read the sidebar on random numbers in Lab 13. *Monte-Carlo* (like the casinos) integration chooses a number n of points to evaluate the function at random, in the interval $x0$ to $x1$. At each point xr, we compute the area of a rectangle of width $h = (x1 - x0)/n$ and height of $f(xr)$. The idea is that the approximation improves as n increases, as long as the random points are evenly spread across the interval.

Implement `integrate-monte`, a Monte-Carlo integration procedure.

PROCEDURE (`integrate-monte` f $x0$ $x1$ n $seed$)

ARGUMENTS
- f is a procedure of one numerical argument that returns a number
- $x0$ is a number that specifies the left end of the range
- $x1$ is a number that specifies the right end of the range
- n is the number of subintervals
- n is a number to seed the random number generator

RETURNS   the approximate area of f from $x0$ using n random points

---

Try Simpson's Rule and Monte Carlo integration on $f(x) = e^x$ between 0 and 4, picking $n = 4$. $\int e^x dx = e^x$ (an amazing fact). Compare the results achieved by each of the numerical methods with the theoretical value $e^4 - e^0 = e^4 - 1$.

Deliverables: listings of `integrate-simp` and `integrate-monte` and listings showing how they work on the examples we used for `integrate-trap`.

Lab 10

Cartesian Computation

Graphing functions by hand is a useful but tedious activity; it became one of the first applications of computer graphics. You will experiment with Scheme's graphics procedures in this lab, as well as seeing the power of procedures as arguments.

WHAT YOU NEED TO KNOW

Read up to the end of Section 3.3. Make sure you understand Scheme's graphics operators.

PROBLEM STATEMENT

In this lab, you are going to write a program that allows you to plot a mathematical function. One way to do this is to identify every value of x you're interested in, and then calculate the corresponding value of y. Then you mark the points on a piece of graph paper, and connect the points. Admittedly, you don't get a smooth curve, but if you choose the values of x to be "close enough", the curve will look fairly smooth.

For example, if we wanted to graph $y = \sqrt{x}$, for $0 \le x \le 100$, we would start at $x = 0$, and get a table something like:

```
0 0
1 1
2 1.414213562373095
3 1.732050807568877
4 2
5 2.23606797749979
6 2.449489742783178
7 2.645751311064591
8 2.82842712474619
9 3
10 3.16227766016838
...
97 9.848857801796104
98 9.899494936611665
99 9.9498743710662
100 10
```

Once we have the table, it's a simple matter to get a piece of graph paper and play connect-the-dots to produce a graph.

The program that produced the above output was:

```
(define tabulate-sqrt
  (lambda (x0 x1)
    (if (> x0 x1)
      (newline)
      (begin
        (format #t "~a ~a~%" x0 (sqrt x0))
        (tabulate-sqrt (add1 x0) x1)))))
```

In this procedure, x0 is the lowest value to tabulate, and x1 is the highest. We evaluated (`tabulate-sqrt 0 100`).

However, instead of producing a table and then drawing the picture by hand, we can use graphics procedures to produce a graph. We will move to $(0, 0)$, draw a small line to $(1, 1)$, and then another small line to $(2, 1.414)$, and so on. If you stand back from the screen, it will look like a smooth curve. That is what we will do in this lab.

BEFORE THE LAB

1. Study `tabulate-sqrt`, and convince yourself that it does indeed work.
2. Using the graphics procedures described in the attached note, produce a procedure called `plot-sqrt` that is like `tabulate-sqrt`, except that it draws a graph.
3. Study our `cube-root` procedure (the one that does it by bisection) and write an analogous `fourth-root` procedure, that is, write a procedure that, given x, finds the positive number z such that $z^4 = x$.

CHECKPOINT

1. What will happen if we evaluate (`cube-root-solve 3 4 10`)?
2. In `factorial`, we used n both as the value that is multiplied by the recursive result (`* n (factorial (sub1 n))`) *and* as the counter that indicated when to stop (`= n 0`). Rewrite `factorial` to use a helper that, keeping n fixed, counts up from 0 to n.
3. Does `fourth-root` have to worry, like `cube-root`, about whether its argument is positive or negative?

DURING THE LAB

1. Type in your `plot-sqrt` procedure, and try it out. Once you have it working, get a printout of both the program and the graph.
2. Make a copy of the file containing `plot-sqrt`, and modify it so that it plots the fourth root function instead. Use the fourth root procedure you wrote before the lab. Again get a printout of both the program and the graph.
3. These two plotting procedures both have the same structure. You can therefore use a procedure that takes a procedure as an argument; the procedure will be called, say, `plot-function`, and should be as follows:

```
(define plot-function
   (lambda (x0 x1 p)
   ...)
```

where p is the name to be used for the procedure that computes the function we want to plot. Use your `plot-function` procedure to plot the square and fourth root functions, as well as $y = 0.3x$ and $y = \log_{10} x$ (Scheme has no base 10 logarithm procedure; however, the procedure `log` gives you the natural—base e—logarithm. You can use the identity $\log_{10} x = \log_e x / \log_e 10$ to write a procedure `log10` that returns the base 10 logarithm of its argument.

AFTER THE LAB

Review your `plot-function` procedure, and convince yourself that it does indeed work, by evaluating (`plot-function 1 5 sqrt`), using 𝕮𝔥𝔢 𝕽𝔲𝔩𝔢𝔰. Show how the application reduces to evaluating the body of the procedure, which is a sequence of forms. 𝕮𝔥𝔢 𝕽𝔲𝔩𝔢𝔰 has no rules for evaluating a sequence of forms, but we can treat a sequence as just evaluating the first, the second, and so forth.

You'll need two columns for your answer, one showing the actual evaluation (using 𝕮𝔥𝔢 𝕽𝔲𝔩𝔢𝔰), and the other shown what is actually drawn. Use abbreviations rather than long procedure names such as `draw-display`. The point here is to show a few steps and to indicate how the series of calls to `plot-function` generates the calls to `draw-move` that plot the function.

DELIVERABLES

1. the listings from your square root, fourth root, and your plotting procedures, along with the graphs produced.
2. your evaluation work from the "After the lab" part, above.
3. anything you've done for the Optional Credit part.

FOR FURTHER INVESTIGATION

The graphs are pretty sparse, without axes or labels. Make your `plot-function` procedure produce an attractive graph with labeled axes, and with a label for the graph. (You might want to use strings here.) The `draw-display` procedure will be particularly useful here. `draw-display` is like `draw-text` except that its argument can be any printable Scheme value. `draw-display` first creates a string that is the printed representation of the value, and then does the same thing as `draw-text`, with that string as input.

Deliverables: a code listing, a transcript, and a printout of the graph

[Involves math] All of these graphs have to live within a 500 by 500 range on the screen. Unfortunately, most interesting functions won't look very good on such a grid. Consider, for example, $y = x^2$. $200^2 = 40000$, which will go way off the screen. Modify your procedure so that it "scales" the y values so that they fit in the window. To do this, you'll need to work out a method of transforming y coordinates so that they fit into the range from 0 to 500. If you do the same with x, you'll be able to plot functions over other ranges, say from -500 to +500, albeit with lower accuracy.

Deliverables: a code listing, a transcript, and a printout of the graph

Lab 11

Graphical Procedures and Operators

This lab is designed to give you a chance to explore procedures as arguments, as well as to explore graphics. We will see how we can define "shape procedures" that define geometric figures of interest and then define "shape operators" that allow us to manipulate these figures in the graphics window.

WHAT YOU NEED TO KNOW

Read the text through the end of Chapter 3.

PROBLEM STATEMENT

We have already seen how to write very specific graphics procedures, for drawing a 100×100 square starting at $(125, 125)$, for example. In this lab, we'll see how to generalize them.

Graphics programs are often designed to draw the same shape over and over again, perhaps located at different places, with different magnifications, and maybe at different angles. We might draw one 50 by 50 square in the lower left corner of the graphics window, another 100 by 100 square in the upper right corner, and a third in the middle, but rotated by 45 degrees. We could write separate procedures for each of these squares, but this would rapidly become tedious.

One way of generalizing the `square` procedure is to give it several parameters. We can pass in the coordinates of two points, as in the following.

```
(define square-x-and-y
  (lambda (x1 y1 x2 y2)
    (begin
      (draw-move x1 y1)
      (draw-line x2 y1)
      (draw-line x2 y2)
      (draw-line x1 y2)
      (draw-line x1 y1))))
```

But as the picture we draw becomes more and more complex, more and more parameters must be added. Rather than have procedures with large numbers of arguments, we would like a more systematic way of attacking this problem. Graphic transformations (see the sidebar) will do the job.

Graphic transformations operate upon pictures. In Scheme, we represent pictures as procedures. Therefore, a graphic transformation will be a procedure that takes a picture procedure as an argument, and returns a new procedure that draws the transformed picture. For example, we will have a `scale` procedure that accepts as an argument our procedure that draws a 1×1 square, and returns a procedure that draws an $n \times n$ square, where n is the scale factor.

Our new `square` procedure looks like this:

```
(define square
  (lambda (mv dr)
    (mv 0 0)
    (dr 0 1)
    (dr 1 1)
    (dr 1 0)
    (dr 0 0)))
```

Graphic Transformations

Suppose you had a piece of transparent rubber with a 1×1 square drawn on it. One point, say the lower-left corner, is known as the **reference point**. Is there any way to use this to make a square of any size, orientation, and location on the plane?

The question itself gives the answer. Since it's a piece of rubber, we can stretch it. We can move the sheet of rubber to align the reference point with any location we want. And we can turn it about the reference point.

We therefore speak of three **graphic transformation operators:**

- **scaling** multiplies the coordinates of each point by a given amount. For our purposes, the x and y coordinates are multiplied by the same **scale factor**

- **translation** moves the figure so that instead of the reference point being at $(0, 0)$, it is at a specified value. During a translation operation, the rubber is not stretched; therefore, each other coordinate will be modified by the same value.

- **rotation** turns the figure around an axis through the reference point by a specified angle.

Only scaling stretches the rubber on which the square is drawn; the other two operators treat the rubber as unstretchable.

Suppose we want a diamond (a slanted square) that is 3×3, with reference point at $(3, 4)$. The picture—created in Adobe Illustrator, which uses these graphical operators as its basic commands—shows how the following sequence of graphical operations does the job.

  a. **create** the unit square
  b. **scale** by 3
  c. **translate** by $(3, 4)$
  d. **rotate** by 45 degrees

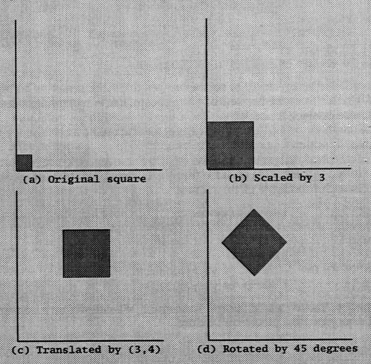

    (a) Original square   (b) Scaled by 3

    (c) Translated by (3,4)   (d) Rotated by 45 degrees

Scale, translate, and rotate are graphical operators. You can think of them as functions that accept shapes as inputs, and that output the transformed shape. Complex transformations can be expressed as combinations of these operators. Graphics languages such as PostScript use this technique not only for pictures, but also for scaling fonts.

This procedure draws a unit square (one with length and width 1), provided it is passed the appropriate arguments:

```
(square draw-move draw-line)
```

But how do we get a square of length and width 100? We don't change `square`; instead, we change its inputs.

```
(square
  (lambda (x y) (draw-move (* 100 x) (* 100 y)))
  (lambda (x y) (draw-line (* 100 x) (* 100 y))))
```

In this call of `square`, `mv` is bound to a procedure that moves to coordinates $(100x, 100y)$; `dr` is bound to a procedure that draws a line to $(100x, 100y)$. `square` thinks it is still drawing a unit square, but the actual draw and move procedures magnify the size of the square. We have "scaled" our square, magnifying it by a factor of 100.

We can make a procedure that produces a scaled square.

```
(define scale-square
  (lambda (s)
    (lambda (mv dr)
      (square
        (lambda (x y) (mv (* s x) (* s y)))
        (lambda (x y) (dr (* s x) (* s y)))))))
```

`scale-square` doesn't draw a square of size s, but returns a procedure that when applied to `draw-move` and `draw-line` draws the square.

We can generalize this to scale any shape procedure:

```
(define scale
  (lambda (p s)
    (lambda (mv dr)
      (p
        (lambda (x y) (mv (* s x) (* s y)))
        (lambda (x y) (dr (* s x) (* s y)))))))
```

The shape procedure is the argument `p`, so we can get the same result as before by `( (scale square 100) draw-move draw-line)`. Notice the two sets of parentheses: `scale` returns a procedure of two arguments, which we then apply to the drawing procedures.

The idea is to take the shape procedure and a scale factor and return a new shape procedure that modifies the `mv` and `dr` procedures by scaling their arguments by s.

The second graphical transformation is translation, which moves a picture (without stretching it) so that the reference point is at (x_1, y_1). Since we assume that the reference point is at $(0, 0)$, translating a picture means adding (x_1, y_1) to each coordinate of the picture.

```
(define translate
  (lambda (p x1 y1)
    (lambda (mv dr)
      (p
        (lambda (x y) (mv (+ x1 x) (+ y1 y)))
        (lambda (x y) (dr (+ x1 x) (+ y1 y)))))))
```

Our pictures expect a "move" and a "draw" procedure. We can define a convenience procedure that passes `draw-move` and `draw-text` to a picture procedure.

```
(define show
  (lambda (p)
    (p draw-move draw-line)))
```

Now we can write the form in the previous problem as `(show (translate square 100 125))`. This is just a bit cleaner.

BEFORE THE LAB

1. Convince yourself that `square-x-and-y` works correctly when we call it with (`square-x-and-y` 10 20 100 200). The best way to convince yourself is to get a piece of graph paper, and "hand simulate" the Scheme evaluator as it does this call.

2. Evaluate (`scale-square` 100). Write a Scheme form that uses this value to draw a (100, 100) square.

3. Write a form that draws a unit square with the reference point at (100, 125).

4. Design a procedure, patterned on `square`, for drawing an equilateral triangle (one with all sides the same length). Two of the vertices will be (0, 0) and (1, 0). Identify the coordinates of the third vertex (both will be positive); if necessary, you might want to do this on graph paper. Write a couple of other shape procedures for other simple figures, such as a plus sign or an isosceles triangle.

5. Evaluate the following and show what gets drawn.

```
((translate square 100 100) draw-move draw-line)
```

CHECKPOINT

1. Under what circumstances will (`bar` 3) cause an error, when bar is defined as

```
(define bar
  (lambda (x)
    (+ y x)))
```

2. What is the value of (`foo` 3), when foo is defined as

```
(define foo
  (lambda (x)
    (lambda (y) (+ y x))))
```

3. How could you get your `square` procedure to draw a rectangle whose x dimension is twice its y dimension?

DURING THE LAB

In each of the following problems, you are asked to produce a drawing. Be sure you include one or more `draw-display` calls to include your name and other information, as well as a brief description of what is being drawn. (This would be a good place to write a procedure! You can make your procedure have a single argument, which would be a string giving the description of the picture. This string argument can be passed to `draw-display`.)

1. Load the procedures given in the previous section. Try them out by writing a procedure that draws a 25 by 25 square with one corner at the origin (0, 0). Your procedure will take no arguments.

2. Because `scale` and `translate` each return the same kind of procedure as the one they are given as an argument (i.e., one that can be applied to a line and a move procedure), we can "cascade" them, that is, we can apply one of them to the output of the other, such as (`show` (`scale` (`translate square` 100 100) 2)). Produce a procedure (of no arguments) that draws a 25 by 25 square with its lower left corner at (100, 100) (the other corner will be at (125, 125)). You may not use `draw-line` or `draw-move` explicitly in your form.

3. Does scaling before translation produce the same result as translation before scaling? Test your theory by inverting the roles of `scale` and `translate` in your solution to the previous problem. Write a new procedure that does this.

4. One of the nicest features of the design of shape procedures is that we can easily build more complex figures out of shape procedure building blocks. For example, a stylized house could be drawn as a square with an equilateral triangle on top. Define a `house` procedure that draws a tiny house, consisting of a unit square with a corresponding equilateral triangle on top. You can't do any explicit line drawing or moving in this procedure. Use `translate` to position the triangle, e.g.,

```
(define house
  (lambda (dr mv)
    ...
```

Now write a procedure that draws a house, scaled by a factor of 25, with the lower left corner at (100, 100).

5. What if we want to combine a particular set of operators? Define a procedure that takes a shape procedure argument, and returns a procedure that draws the shape scaled by a factor of 25 and translated to (100, 100). Test your procedure on your square and equilateral triangle procedures, as well as the other shape procedures you wrote.

AFTER THE LAB

1. Write a brief (half a page or so) report that answers the question of whether scaling followed by translation is the same as translation followed by scaling. Your answer should explain the results you obtained above, obviously. Briefly describe those results, and state your conclusion. Then give arguments that support your conclusion.

2. Briefly explain what will happen if we scale by a negative factor.

DELIVERABLES

1. listings of the code, Scheme dialogs, and graphics printout for each problem.
2. your answers to the "After the lab" questions.

FOR FURTHER INVESTIGATION

There is one other operator we will need if we want to have a complete set: rotation. This can be accomplished by using a bit of trigonometry. If we want to rotate a figure by an angle θ, we can modify the x and y values according to the values of $\cos \theta$ and $\sin \theta$, respectively. Define a `rotate` operator that accepts a shape procedure by θ degrees, and use it to draw a house that has been rotated by 45 degrees. Write a second procedure that scales its shape procedure argument by 100, then translates it to (50, 50), and finally rotates it by 60 degrees. Apply this procedure to your `house` procedure. Note: this problem will require that you do a bit of math.

The Scheme procedures `sin` and `cos` may be useful here. They take arguments in radians, not degrees. (Hence $(\sin \pi) = 0$.)

Deliverables: Hand in a listing of the code, Scheme dialogs, and graphics printout produced.

Pairs, Boxes and Lists

OBJECTIVES

This lab helps you understand box-and-arrow diagrams and how to access list structures. As well as displaying data structures, box-and-arrow diagrams are very useful in writing list procedures.

The lab has two parts: playing with list structures to learn how they are composed, and writing a few list processing procedures.

WHAT YOU NEED TO KNOW

Read Chapter 4 up through Section 4.3. To do this lab you need to understand pairs, symbols, lists, and box-and-arrow diagrams.

PROBLEM STATEMENT

In the **box-and-arrow** representation, we show a pair as two adjacent boxes, the left for the car and the right for the cdr. The rules for drawing box-and-arrow diagrams are:

- If a box contains another pair, the pair is drawn outside the box, and an arrow connects the first box to the pair contained in it.
- If a box contains any other Scheme value, the value is shown inside the box, if it fits. Otherwise, the value is drawn outside the box, connected by an arrow.

These rules say how to arrange boxes and their contents. The arrows put the contents of some of the boxes outside the boxes so that the diagrams are easier to read. The rule about drawing items outside a box is only for convenience. If the item can fit in the box, put it there.

Here's a hint on how to produce box-and-arrow diagrams for lists: (list v_1 v_2 ... v_n) creates n boxes and puts each of v_i in the left hand side of the boxes and links the right hand side of each box to the next pair. The null list appears in the right hand side of the last box. Remember: (list 1 2 3 4) is equivalent to (cons 1 (cons 2 (cons 3 (cons 4 '())))), and each cons in a form creates a box.

List structures

Here's a few examples of list structures and their box-and-arrow diagrams:

1. (cons 'a 'c) ⇒ (a . c)

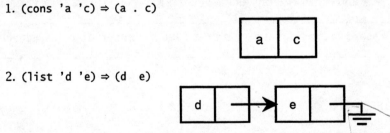

2. (list 'd 'e) ⇒ (d e)

The problems in the lab will ask you to determine the value of some Scheme forms and draw their box-and-arrow diagrams.

Rotating a list

The procedure rotate rotates a list left or right, depending on its second argument. When a list rotates *right*, the rightmost element is removed and becomes the first element. When a list rotates *left*, the leftmost element is removed and becomes the last element.

```
> (rotate '(1 2 3 4 5) 'l)
(2 3 4 5 1)
> (rotate '(1 2 3 4 5) 'r)
(5 1 2 3 4)
```

Compare the structure of the input list with the resulting list.

PROCEDURE (rotate *l sym*)

ARGUMENTS
- *l* is a non-empty list
- *sym* is the symbol r or l.

RETURNS   a list rotated left if *sym* is l or right if *sym* is r.

One of these directions is relatively simple, because car returns the first element of a list and cdr the remaining elements. The other direction is not so simple. It helps to write a separate procedure for that direction.

Selecting items in a list structure

list-ref is useful because it lets us access the top-level elements of a list. (list-ref l n) performs *n* cdr operations, then one car operation.

We can write a more general list access procedure, navigate, that performs a sequence of car and cdr operations. For example, we could specify 2 car operations followed by 1 cdr operation as (a 2 d 1); the a stands for car and the d for cdr.

Here's how we use navigate:

```
> (navigate '(1 2 3 4 5) '(d 3 a 1))
4
> (navigate '((1 2) 3) '(a 2))
1
> (navigate '((1 2) 3) '(a 1 d 1 a 1))
2
> (navigate '(3 (1 2)) '(d 1 a 1))
(1 2)
```

PROCEDURE (navigate *l comms*)

ARGUMENTS
- *l* is a list
- *comms* is a list of alternating symbols and numbers—the symbols are a or d, and the number are non-negative integers

RETURNS   the value got by applying car and cdr operations as in *comms*

It makes sense to write the helpers ncars and ncdrs that perform *n* car and *n* cdr operations, respectively.

PROCEDURE (ncars *l n*)

ARGUMENTS
- *l* is a list
- *n* is a nonnegative integer

RETURNS   the result of applying car *n* times to *l*.

PROCEDURE (ncdrs *l n*)

ARGUMENTS
- *l* is a list
- *n* is a nonnegative integer

RETURNS   the result of applying cdr *n* times to *l*.

Creating duplicate elements in a list

We can write a procedure (duplicate l a n) that creates a new list where every occurrence of a in l is replaced by *n* copies of a.

```
> (duplicate '(1 2 3 4) 3 4)
(1 2 3 3 3 3 4)
> (duplicate '(1 2 3 4 5 4) 4 3)
(1 2 3 4 4 4 5 4 4 4)
```

PROCEDURE (duplicate *l a n*)

ARGUMENTS
- *l* is a list
- *a* is a Scheme value
- *n* is an integer

RETURNS   a new list where every occurrence of *a* in *l* is replaced by *n* copies of *a*

It's best to use a helper, repeat, to create *n* copies of a, when needed, and connect them to the recursive result of duplicate on the rest of the list.

BEFORE THE LAB

1. For the following forms, determine how they are printed out by Scheme, and then draw the box-and-arrow diagram representing the list structure.
    a. (cons 'a (list 'd 'e))
    b. (cons 'a (cons 'b 'c))
    c. (cons (list 'd 'e) 'a)
    d. (append (list 'a) (list 'd))
    e. (append (list 'a) (list 'd 'e))
       Write a sentence comparing this structure with (a).
    f. First evaluate (define foo (cons 'a (list 'd 'e))). Then show the value and draw the box-and-arrow diagram of (car foo).
    g. (cdr foo)
    h. (car (cdr foo))
    i. First evaluate (define bar (cons (list 'a 'b) '(c d))). Then show the value and draw the box-and-arrow diagram of bar.
    j. (cdr (car bar))
    k. First evaluate (define baz (list (list 'a 'b) '(c d))). Then show the value and draw the box-and-arrow diagram of baz.
    l. (cdr (car (cdr baz)))
2. Design rotate as well as test inputs that demonstrate that it works. What are the important cases?
3. Design navigate and its helpers ncars and ncdrs, as well as test inputs that demonstrate that they work.
4. Design duplicate and its helper repeat, as well as test inputs that demonstrate that they work.

PITFALLS AND ADVICE

If you have problems debugging your procedures, write down the box-and-arrow diagrams of the input list and follow the car and cdr operations performed by your list procedure. Use `trace` to determine the effects of the operations. You can compare the box-and-arrow diagrams of the arguments shown by tracing with what you expect from the specification of the procedure.

CHECKPOINT

1. What is the value of (append '(1 2 3 4) 5)?
2. What is the value of (append 5 '(1 2 3 4))?
3. What is the value of (navigate '((1 2) (1 2 (3))) '(d 1 a 1 d1))?

DURING THE LAB

1. Type in the test forms in Problem 1 (a-l) and verify your predictions.
2. Type in `rotate` and test it.
3. Type in `navigate`, `ncars`, and `ncdrs` and test them.
4. Type in `duplicate` and `repeat` and test them.

AFTER THE LAB

Define a list structure x such that (navigate x '(d 2 a 1)) works, but (navigate x '(d 3 a 1)) doesn't.

DELIVERABLES

1. For each (a-l) of the forms in "Before the Lab" part 1, the value and the box-and-arrow diagram
2. a listing of the procedures `rotate`, `navigate`, and `duplicate` and whatever helpers you have used
3. a transcript showing that each of the list procedures works
4. the answer to the "After the lab" question

FOR FURTHER INVESTIGATION

Write a procedure (choose n l) that returns a list of all the lists of length n that can be chosen from the list l, without replacement. For example:

```
> (choose 2 '(a b c d))
((a b) (a c) (a d) (b c) (b d) (c d))
> (choose 1 '(b c d))
((b) (c) (d))
> (choose 0 '(a b c d))
(())                    ;;; there is one way to choose no things
> (choose 5 '(a b c d))
()                      ;;; but there are no ways to choose five things
```

In this problem, the order of the elements is unimportant, so the list (a b) is the same as (b a).

PROCEDURE (choose *n l*)

ARGUMENTS
- *n* is the length of the new lists made of elements selected from *l*
- *l* is a list

RETURNS   the list of all lists of length *n* made up of elements from *l*

Hint: Consider the relationship between the output of choose and the output with various smaller arguments, i.e., with n smaller, or the list reduced by one element.

Deliverables: a program listing and printout

Lab 13

A Word Game

This lab helps you understand strings and lists, how to search them and how to manipulate them, by writing the support procedures for an interactive game based on words.

WHAT YOU NEED TO KNOW

Read the text through Chapter 4. Make sure you understand list procedures.

PROBLEM STATEMENT

This lab leads you to construct a program that plays the **changer** game. The two players are you and the game program. The game program presents two words to you, the **source** and the **goal**, chosen from a dictionary of all three-letter words. The source can be changed into the goal word by a series of one-letter changes, each of which results in a dictionary word. For example, the source hut and goal mug are connected by hut, but, bug and mug. Another chain of words connecting them is hut, hat, rat, rag, rug and mug.

The basic operation in the game is changing one letter in a word. A *successor* of a word is a new word in the dictionary that differs only by one letter from the old word.

In each round of the game, you take the current word (initially the source) and try to change it into the goal. You enter the word. If your word is the goal, you win. Otherwise, the program finds a random successor of your word and presents it to you as the new source. The game continues until your word is the goal, and is a successor of the current source, or you run out of tries. A word can't be used twice in the game.

The dialog in one game is shown in Figure 13-1. Your input is displayed as *hub*. You type a new word at enter:. On the next line, the game prints its choice.

You won, but it took several tries. The game noticed several things:

1. tab is not a successor of hub—it's in the dictionary but differs by more than one letter

2. sun has been used already

3. pur is not a successor of pun, since it's not in the dictionary

In each case it asks you to enter a new word, using the current source.

(games path-length steps random-number) starts the game.

The game program must make many random choices. It first initializes the random number generator. It then chooses a source at random from its list of words. Then it generates a *path*, a list of words each of which is successor to the previous word. The number of words in the path is path-length. No word appears more than once in the list. The last word of the path is the goal. It presents the goal and the source to you and then starts a process of rounds. In each round you enter a successor of the source, until that word is the goal and has not been used before, either by you or the game program. The program lets you have a limited number of tries.

In this lab we'll implement the changer game. We will provide a dictionary, dict, of all three-letter words. Each word is represented by a string, and the dictionary is a list of strings arranged in alphabetical order.

The operation of determining whether one word is a successor of another is expensive. How expensive? A successor must be in the dictionary and differ only by one letter. The first operation depends on the length of the dictionary (about 600), the second on the length of the words (3). Each round of the game requires determining whether a word is a successor. Also, generating a path requires computing successors many times. To speed this up, we will provide suckers, a sorted list of successor lists. A *successor list* is in the form (word succ1 succ2 ... succn), where (succ1 succ2 ... succn) is the list of successors of word. suckers is

```
Thinking ...Goal: mug
source:   hut
enter: hug
 source:  hub
enter: tab
not a successor, try again
 source:  hub
enter: tub
 source:  sub
enter: sun
 source:  pun
enter: sun
good entry, but already used, try again
source:   pun
enter: pur
not a successor, try again --- Hey, not even a word!
 source:  pun
enter: pug
 source:  dug
enter: mug
******* You win! ***********
```

Figure 13-1   A dialog with the game program

sorted by word, in alphabetical order. Each word in a successor list differs in one character from word, and appears in the dictionary. One of our tasks in this lab will be to write the code to create suckers.

The goodie containing the game code is game.scm. It contains the framework of the changer game, omitting some necessary procedures that you will write.

String differences

You will write a procedure (successor? s1 s2) that determines whether the number of characters that differ (position by position) between two strings s1 and s2 is 1.

PROCEDURE (successor? *s1 s2*)

ARGUMENTS
- *s1* is a string
- *s2* is a string

RETURNS   a Boolean indicating whether the difference is 1.

There are a variety of ideas that can lead to a solution. First, you could count the number of different chars in s1 and s2 and then determine whether the result is 1, using a helper, (difference-s s1 s2).

PROCEDURE (difference-s *s1 s2*)

ARGUMENTS
- *s1* is a string
- *s2* is a string

RETURNS   the number of different characters in the strings.

The issues of such an implementation might be:
- string recursion
- what must be computed when s1 runs out
- what must be computed when s2 runs out
- what happens when the characters at position pos are different
- what happens when the characters at position pos are the same

Random numbers

A *random number generator* is a procedure that gives you back a different number each time. If you look at the numbers returned, you'll see there's no apparent regularity—the numbers seem to be drawn at random from a fixed range of numbers, as if the computer were flipping a coin or rolling a die. Actually, a well-defined algorithm produces the numbers. However, the numbers returned by a well-designed random number generator behave as randomly (statistically) as rolling (honest) dice.

Scheme has a procedure (random n) that generates a random integer between 0 and n−1. The numbers generated by successive calls to (random n) are not really random, they just seem that way.

The following procedure, roll-die, makes a list of *m* random numbers:

```
;;; return a list of m rolls of a die.  The result
;;; returned by  random is a number between 0 and n-1 (n=6
;;; here). Since most dice start counting from 1, we add 1
;;; to the result.
(define roll-die
  (lambda (m)
    (if (= 0 m)
        '()
        (cons (add1 (random 6)) (roll-die (sub1 m))))))
> (roll-die 10)
(3 2 3 2 1 3 6 6 6 6)
> (roll-die 10)
(6 1 1 4 6 3 1 4 1 2)
```

When roll-die is evaluated a second time a new list results. After looking at these results, you might be tempted to bet on 6. However, if you just roll an (honest) die a small number of times, you do tend to get behavior like this. It's only when you roll the die hundreds or thousands of times that the number of occurrences of different numbers tends to even out. Statisticians call this the "Law of Large Numbers."

In Scheme we can get the same random sequence at different times by calling the procedure (random-seed seed), where seed is a 6 or more digit number chosen randomly (by you!). The argument seed makes the random-picture repeatable (for debugging) and changeable (you can pass in your favourite number, the time of day (in decimal), or anything). Try this out: evaluate (random-seed *your-favourite-number*), then (random 1000) several times. Each time you evaluate (random 1000), you'll get a different number in the range 0–999. Evaluate (random-seed *your-favourite-number*) again, and then (random 1000) will begin that (apparently) random sequence again.

You can assume that the strings are the same length, since this game handles only three-letter words.

A second implementation could count the number of different chars in s1 and s2. While counting, if the number greater becomes than 1, return #f. This procedure could also use string recursion.

Successors

The procedure success constructs the list of successors for a word. The global variable dict contains the sorted list of words. success is used in creating suckers.

PROCEDURE (success *word dict*)

ARGUMENTS
- *word* is a string
- *dict* is the dictionary, a list of strings

RETURNS   the successor list for *word*

What's needed? The word must be compared with every word in the dictionary. Only those are kept for which successor? returns #t.

Searching successor lists

We need a procedure `search-suckers` to search the list of successors, `suckers`, to find the successors of a word. `suckers` is a global variable.

PROCEDURE (`search-suckers` *sym*)

ARGUMENTS
- *sym* is a string

RETURNS   the list of successors of word, or () if *sym* is not in `suckers`

Selecting strings randomly

We need a procedure (`select-new strings old`) that selects, at random, an element in `strings`, a list of strings, that does not appear in `old`, a list of strings. The game uses `select-new` when producing a new source word. It maintains the list of words already used, `old`. `strings` is the successors of the word you have typed in.

PROCEDURE (`select-new` *strings old*)

ARGUMENTS
- *strings* is a list of strings
- *old* is the list of used strings

RETURNS   a random element of *strings* not in *old*, or #f if there is no element in *strings* not in *old*.

There are two ways to write `select-new`:
1. Remove all words in `old` from `strings`. Select one of the remaining words at random.
2. Select a word in `strings` at random. If it's in `old`, remove it from `strings` and try again, until you find one not in `old`.

   You can use the procedure `remove` in the goodie:

PROCEDURE (`remove` *item lst*)

ARGUMENTS
- *item* is the item to be removed
- *lst* is the list from which *item* is to be removed

RETURNS   a copy of *lst* from which *item* has been removed

Generating sequences of successor strings

The main procedure for creating the list of words in the game is (`generate len`), a procedure that creates a path of length `len`.

PROCEDURE (`generate` *len*)

ARGUMENTS
- *len* is the length of the path

RETURNS   a list containing *len* strings (*len* is the length of the desired list), each a successor of the previous

---

`generate` must choose a word to start (the source), at random, from the available words in `suckers`. Then its helper `genpath` creates the path of length `len-1` from the successor list of the source, with an initial path that is the list containing the source.

PROCEDURE (genpath *sx len acc*)

ARGUMENTS
- *sx* is the successor list of the current word
- *len* the length of the remaining path
- *acc* is the current path

RETURNS   a list of strings, each a successor of the previous

---

The example we showed at the beginning had the source hut and the goal mug. One of many paths between hut and mug is hut, rut, rug, and mug. In building the path, we'd like to get a more or less difficult path by avoiding coming back to the words already used. Of course, one of the successors of rut is hut. So it can't be used. This simple rule helps create interesting games, but isn't enough by itself to guarantee a good game: hug is one of the successors of rug and doesn't appear in the path, but it is also a successor of hut. The "Further Investigations" section shows you how to create even more difficult games.

genpath must choose a word w in the list sx. A word can't appear twice in the list, so w can't be in acc. You've already designed a procedure to handle this kind of selection. Use it. genpath adds w to acc, and recurses, with a new sx that is the successor list of w. The new length is now len-1. genpath returns acc when len is 0.

Sometimes the path has a "dead end". The current source either has no successor or it has no successor that is not already in the path. Then genpath must return #f. generate returns the result of genpath. When the result is #f, its caller must try again, with a new random number seed.

BEFORE THE LAB

1. Write a module containing the procedures to support the game: successor?, success, search-suckers, select-new, generate, and genpath. The procedure difference-s is optional, but we suggest you write and use it.

CHECKPOINT

1. Would symbols be a useful representation for words in this lab?
2. What would be another possible representation for words, besides strings, in this lab?
3. What is the value of (successor? "foo" "ofo")?

DURING THE LAB

1. The goodie containing the game code is in game.scm. Load it first, since it contains the small dictionary, mini, and list of successors.
2. in the procedures you have designed and test them using the test values you have chosen. The goodie provides a small dictionary mini for testing your success procedure. Using the full dictionary dict takes too long.
3. Try to run the game by using your procedures. You start the game by typing:

   (games len steps a-random-number)

   where len is the length of the path, steps is the number of tries you get, and a-random-number is a number of your choosing to seed the random number generator.

AFTER THE LAB

1. There were several alternative designs in the lab. Compare them; in each case, which is better? Are some of the designs better with respect to complexity, clarity, or ease of programming?
2. How would you write a program to play this game?
3. How could the game program be tougher, that is, how could it make it harder for you to win?

DELIVERABLES

1. a listing the module containing your procedures: `successor?`, `success`, `search-suckers`, `select-new`, `generate`, and `genpath`

2. a transcript showing that the procedures work individually, and that the game works with them

3. answers to the "After the Lab" questions

FOR FURTHER INVESTIGATION

Write `generate-hard`, a version of `generate` that ensures that none of the words in the path is a successor of any other word in the path but the immediately previous word. It should have the same structure as `genpath`. It must choose `w` from `sx`, that is not in `acc`, but `w` must also not be a successor of any of the words in `acc`. The path `hut`, `rut`, `rug`, and `hug` is acceptable for `genpath` but not for `genpath-hard`, since `hug` is a successor of `hut`.

There are two alternatives. You could maintain the list of all successors of words in `acc` as you build `acc`, or you could create this list each time you consider a new word.

Deliverables: a listing of your program and a printout showing that it works

Lab 14
That Long-Distance Feeling

OBJECTIVES

Programs use data structures such as lists to represent real-world data. This lab is designed to give you practice building a program that uses list structure for two purposes: representing values of an ADT, and representing a collection of values.

WHAT YOU NEED TO KNOW

Before attempting this lab, you should have read up to the end of Chapter 4.

PROBLEM STATEMENT

Ruritanian Telephone and Television (RT&T) provides a long-distance service to its customers. Each time a customer makes a long-distance call, a record is generated by the switch[1] connected to the caller's phone. Periodically, the call records are collected and prepared into a bill for the customer. It is our job to write the billing program. Its input is the customers' call records, and it prints the bill for each customer.

The Customer File

Your program will process a file of customers, each of which has zero or more call records. A call record looks like

> (*area-code exchange number date start-time end-time*)

An example is

> (416 555 1234 "94.12.08" 0752 0803)

Calling times are recorded to the nearest minute. (Time is represented as an integer *hour* + 100 * *minutes*.) You can assume that no call lasts 24 hours or more.

Before our program has been run, the call records have been collected and organized by customer, into records that look like

> *area-code exchange number customer-name*
>   *call-record* ...
>   end

The entire customer file is ended with the symbol end-of-data. (end and end-of-data are **sentinels**, data values that indicate the end of a group of data.) An example of a customer file is shown in Figure 14-1.

The basic cost of a call is set by the area code. For example, calling from area code 604 (Southwestern British Columbia), the rate might be 17 cents per minute to area code 206 (Western Washington), or 35 cents per minute to area code 212 (Manhattan).

---

[1] Telephone lines are connected to a device known as a **switch**. It is this device that decodes the desired phone number and makes the call for the customer. Early telephone systems used human operators, who would physically wire the caller's and callee's telephones together, using a patch cord. In the 1930s, a Kansas City funeral director named Strowger developed an electro-mechanical switch that replaced the operator. The Strowger switch remained in wide use until it was replaced by electronic switches (first analog and then digital) decades later. Modern telephone switches are computer-based. A switch might correspond to a telephone exchange, e.g., 435-*xxxx*; large organizations use a private branch exchange (PBX), another kind of switch.

```
604 555 4578 "Chandler, Ruth"
(604 555 2953 "94.12.02" 1305 1317)
(808 555 3061 "94.12.05" 2357 0004)
(416 555 4830 "94.12.25" 0905 0917)
end
604 555 2233 "Thompson, Jeff"
(212 555 8765 "94.12.17" 0932 0935)
(206 555 0123 "94.12.22" 1715 1721)
end
end-of-data
```

Figure 14-1   A sample customer file

The problem is complicated by the elaborate system of discounts RT&T provides. All calls between 18:00 and 22:59 are discounted 35%; calls between 23:00 and 07:59 are discounted 60%. (The applicable discount is determined by the *starting* time of the call.) Further, if the total cost of all calls is greater than $25.00 after these discounts, then there is a further 10% discount to all calls to other area codes (there is no discount to calls in the customer's area code.) Pay attention to formatting the bills correctly. Calls should be listed by date, and by starting time if there is more than one call on a given day. A sample bill might look like

```
(604) 555-4578        Chandler, Ruth

  ...Call to...    ..Date..    ...Time...  Min Dsc  Cost  You Save
  (604) 555-2953    94.12.02    1305 1317   12   0   1.20  0.00
  (808) 555-3061    94.12.05    2357 0004    7  60   1.40  2.10
  (416) 555-4830    94.12.25    0905 0917   12   0   4.20  0.00

                                      Total 6.80  2.10
                        Out-of-area discount 0.00
                           Balance owing 6.80
```

(Some versions of format aren't very accommodating, and don't give you control over the exact number of decimal places. Your instructor might have a suggestion on this. If not, you might have to put up with a less pleasant looking bill.)

Strategy

Solving this problem well requires the use of data abstraction. A data type call-record will allow us to manage information about each call, and a data type customer can manage the information about customers and their calls.

The call-record type should support
- a *read procedure* that reads one call record in
- a *display procedure* that writes out a call record in a readable format
- an *accessor* that returns the area code for the call
- an *accessor* that returns the number of minutes for the call
- an *accessor* that returns the discount percentage (0 to 100%) for the call.

The customer type should support:
- a *read procedure* that reads in one customer record
- a *display procedure* that shows the basic customer information (but not the phone call information)
- a *mapping procedure* that applies the procedure given as its argument to each phone call, and returns a list of the results of each call to the argument procedure

The data structure of the call records is hidden inside the customer type. Any time we need to process the call record data, we can use the mapping procedure to produce a list of whatever values we need for each call in order to carry out the task at hand. For example, (the-customer 'map-calls cost-of-a-call) will evaluate to a list of cost values, assuming that the procedure cost-of-a-call accepts a single call record and computes the cost.

With these two data types, the main procedure should be fairly straightforward to write. You will need a loop for each customer, a procedure for calculating the cost of a call, and a procedure for computing the out-of-area discount.

For computing the cost per minute to a given area code, you might plan to use a complicated if:

```
(if (= code 416)
  35
  (if (= code 808)
    35
    (if (= code 206)
      17
      ...
```

There's a better way: we can represent the information in a table where for each code we record the cost per minute. We can implement the table as a list of pairs. The car of each pair will be the area code, and the cdr will be the cost per minute. Such a list might look like

```
( (416 . 35) (808 . 35) (206 . 17) ... )
```

All that is then needed is a procedure that scans this list, looking for a pair whose car is equal to our area code. The cdr of the pair is the cost per minute. (This structure is an example of an **association list**, or **alist**. We shall study alists in detail in Chapter 5.)

One other matter should be resolved: where the data is. We are going to use two data files: one will contain the customer and call data, and the other will contain the area code cost data. `with-input-from-file` can be used to read these files.

BEFORE THE LAB

1. Compute Jeff Thompson's phone bill.
2. Create your own test data file, following the format shown in this lab. Your test data file should not have Ruth's or Jeff's data in it, but should have enough customers and types of call records to test for each special case. Compute the bills for the customers.
3. Write specifications for the procedures for the `customer` and `call-record` data types.
4. Write the read and display procedures for the `call-record` data type.
5. Write the `call-record` procedure that computes the length of a call. You will need a procedure that computes the difference between two times. Remember that there are 60, not 100, minutes in an hour, and that a call that starts at 2359 and ends at 0001 lasts for two minutes. You might want to use the `daytime` Abstract Data Type from Lab 8.
6. Write the remaining `call-record` procedures. Build a module that exports these procedures.
7. Write a module that exports the `customer` procedures.

PITFALLS AND ADVICE

1. Reading data is always somewhat tricky. When you start to read a data element, you might get a sentinel instead. Be careful to check for the sentinel after you have read the first data value. (Don't try to read a customer's phone number and name and *then* check for the sentinel.) A good idea is to design the input procedures to return either a valid data value or #f if a sentinel was read.
2. You will probably want to organize your input procedures with `let` forms. This is a good idea, but watch out for the order of evaluation. If you are going to read several items in a single form, using `let*` instead of `let` will get rid of the order-of-evaluation problems.

CHECKPOINT

1. Draw a box-and-arrow diagram of Ruth Chandler's billing data. Identify on the diagram each of the call records.
2. Write a procedure that finds the number of minutes in the longest single call for a customer (for Ruth, that will be 12 minutes). Your procedure should accept as an argument the customer, and should use the mapping procedure defined for customers.
3. Write a procedure that is given a customer and that returns a list of all of the out-of-area code calls.

DURING THE LAB

1. Type in your `call-record` module. Write a short test program that tests the data type thoroughly. Get a printout of this test program and put it aside.
2. Now type in the `customer-record` module. Again, test them thoroughly, and put the results aside.
3. Finally, build a main program that repetitively reads customer data from a file, and produces customer bills. Test it interactively.
4. Now test your main program with the test data file you have prepared, and check that the program is correct. Did you check all the boundary cases?

AFTER THE LAB

1. We made some assumptions in order to simplify the problem. Assuming RT&T's rate structure (i.e., don't complicate the discount algorithm), list and explain five assumptions we've made. Briefly describe, in a sentence or two, how we could modify the program to remove each of these assumptions.
2. Suppose that we had used procedural abstraction, rather than data abstraction, in our design for this program. What sorts of problems will arise when we go to modify the program? Give specific examples. Hint: sketch out a procedural design for the program before you try to answer this question.

DELIVERABLES

1. a listing of the `call-record` procedures and the test program
2. a listing of the `customer-record` procedures and their tests
3. a listing of your main program and its tests
4. the answer to the "After the Lab" questions

Lab 15

A Picture Language

OBJECTIVES

Languages are data that is interpreted by a program. When you enter a Scheme program, you put it into a file, and then load it into the evaluator. A program in any programming language is data for the evaluator for that language. We can build languages for many purposes. For example, a picture language would define shapes by "forms" in that language. We can represent a picture as a list of commands that draw the elements of the picture. In this lab, you will build a evaluator for a picture language. Not only will you see the relationship between a language and its evaluator; you will also strengthen your abilities in list processing as you implement the picture language.

WHAT YOU NEED TO KNOW

Read up through Section 4.3 in the text. Make sure you understand list creation and access.

PROBLEM STATEMENT

In Lab 11 we implemented procedures to draw particular shapes, and to scale and translate these shapes on the screen. We can generalize this idea, thinking of a picture as a collection of commands that draw the picture. You will be building a program to draw a picture by executing those commands.

In our language, a picture is represented as a list of commands; each command is a list with three elements, for example, (move x y) or (draw x y). The first element is either move or draw, and the second and third elements are x and y coordinates.

You are going to write, in Scheme, a program that "understands" specifications in a new language, the picture language. For example, a series of commands that draws a square of side length 100 at (0, 0) is:

```
(define square-pic
  '((move 0 0)
    (draw 100 0)
    (draw 100 100)
    (draw 0 100)
    (draw 0 0)))
```

square-pic is just a list, but you can regard that list as a list of *commands*. Your program will look at each command, and carry it out.

The drawing program for the pictures, draw-picture, is a recursive procedure that steps down the list of commands, evaluating each command in turn. When it encounters a move command it moves the point on the screen to the specified coordinates. When it sees a draw command, it must draw a line from the present position to the point specified by (x,y).

To test out the procedures you write to implement the drawing program, we'll need some way to generate large classes of pictures. We'll use the ability of computers to create random numbers. (See the sidebar on random numbers in Lab 13.)

To generate random pictures, we need random numbers for three purposes:

1. to specify the number of commands in the picture
2. to decide, for each command, whether the command is move or draw
3. to generate random points

You'll want the fraction (between 0 and 1) of the commands that are draw instead of move to be greater than 0.5, probably greater than 0.75. To make a random choice, you'll need to have a parameter `fraction` and some code like

```
(if (< (random 1000) (* fraction 1000))
    {generate a draw}
    {generate a move}
)
```

`(random 1000)` will return a number between 0 and 999. If you make `fraction` relatively small, say 0.1, then the probability of getting a random number less than fraction×1000 is only 0.1, which means that in most cases we'll generate moves. Change `fraction` to a large number, say 0.9, and most of the commands will be draws.

Picture manipulation

Now that we know how to draw, and create random pictures, let's manipulate the pictures. We'll write procedures `scale`, `translate`, and `reflect`. The first two are familiar from Lab 11. Reflection about the *x* axis, for example, does not affect the *x* coordinate, but changes the *y* coordinate from positive to negative and vice-versa. Draw a triangle on a piece of graph paper, and reflect it about first the *x* and then the *y* axis in order to see what's going on.

Your `reflect` procedure will take a picture and an argument to indicate whether to reflect about the *x* or *y* axis. That second argument will be either the symbol *x* or the symbol *y*, as appropriate. (In the example, we quote this argument. If we had left off the quote symbol, then we would have got an error telling us that *x* was unbound.)

```
(reflect square-pic 'y) =>
  ((move 0 0)
   (draw -100 0)
   (draw -100 100)
   (draw 0 100)
   (draw 0 0))
```

`reflect` doesn't draw anything; it returns a picture list.

Extending the picture language

Our picture language requires that we write out each step of the picture as a command. We have already learned that when programming in Scheme we use procedures to allow us to break problems down into pieces

Representing commands   A command is a list with three elements, so you could use `car`, `cdr`, and `cons` to access the three elements. A better way of doing this is to implement an ADT for commands. We will implement a constructor, `make-command`, and a set of accessors: `command-name`, `command-x`, and `command-y`. When you are putting together a list of items it's easiest to use the Scheme procedure `list`.

Constructor
- (make-command *name x-coord y-coord*)
  Return a new command with the specified components.

Accessors
- (command-name *command*)
  Return the name of *command*.
- (command-x *command*)
  Return the *x* coordinate of *command*.
- (command-y *command*)
  Return *y* coordinate of *command*.

Figure 15-1   **Abstract Data Type:** command

Drawing a picture   draw-picture works on a list of commands, so the skeleton is:

```
(define draw-picture
  (lambda (pic)
    (if ...
      (begin
        (do-command (... pic))
        (draw-picture ...)))))
```

draw-picture returns no result; it is only evaluated for its effect, not its answer.

You'll also have to write do-command, the procedure that executes one single command.

Creating random pictures   The procedure random-picture creates random input for draw-picture.

PROCEDURE (random-picture *seed fraction size number*)

ARGUMENTS
- *seed* is a 6 or more digit number (this will be the seed)
- *fraction* is a number between 0 and 1 that specifies the proportion of draw commands
- *size* is the maximum coordinate size
- *number* is the number of commands in the picture

RETURNS   a random picture with *number* commands

Transforming pictures   We need picture transformation procedures. The procedure scale-command scales one picture command by a given value. For example,

```
(scale-command '(move 10 10) 2) ⇒ (move 20 20)
```

We also need similar procedures for translation and reflection.

The procedures to transform pictures use the appropriate -command procedures.

- (scale picture factor), where factor is an integer.
- (translate picture x y), where x y are offsets in *x, y* to be added to each point in the picture.
- (reflect picture axis), where axis is 'x or 'y, indicating the *x* or *y* axis.

scale-command and scale are different: the former works only on a single command; the latter uses scale-command to work its way through an entire picture (i.e., a list of commands).

BEFORE THE LAB

1. Design and write a module that implements the command ADT module for pictures.
2. Design and write a module that contains the procedures for manipulating commands: scale-command, translate-command, and reflect-command. Your module will make use of the command ADT module.
3. Design and write a module that manipulates and draws pictures. Your module will define scale, translate, and reflect, as well as draw-picture.
4. Write the procedure random-picture.

CHECKPOINT

1. Give a form using only cons that creates the list (x y).
2. What kind of number will the result of (/ (random 1000) 1000) be? Write another Scheme form to compute (< (random 1000) (* fraction 1000)).
3. Can you write reflect using scale? If not, how would you change scale to let you write reflect?

DURING THE LAB

In each of the following problems, you are asked to produce a drawing. Be sure you include one or more draw-display calls to include your name and other information, and a brief description of what is being drawn.

1. Type in your modules. Try out the command ADT, and make sure it works.
2. Define two pictures by hand and draw them using draw-picture. Get a listing of your procedures and your two pictures, and plots of the 2 pictures.
3. Type in your random-picture procedure. Get a listing of the procedure and a plot of a random picture.
4. Test the module containing scale, translate, and reflect to take pictures as arguments and return new pictures. Show that they work by demonstrating their operation on a picture. Print the results.

AFTER THE LAB

1. Briefly explain what will happen if we apply the list procedure reverse to a picture.
2. Our design for picture commands uses draw and move, but these units may be too small for a useful language. What if our list of picture commands was dropped and became scrambled? Design a new command that would "stand alone". Each command would be independent of the one before.

DELIVERABLES

1. listings of all your modules, and a listing of random-picture
2. transcripts and drawing printouts that demonstrate that your works
3. your answers to the "After the Lab" question

FOR FURTHER INVESTIGATION

We'd like to implement "procedures" in our picture language. First, we'll add the command subpicture to our language. To handle this command, we'll preprocess a picture using (expand-picture *picture insert*), where *picture* is a picture, possibly with occurrences of subpicture in the description, and *insert* is a picture without any occurrences of subpicture. expand-picture returns a new picture with all occurrences of the command subpicture replaced by the picture *insert*. Then, the expanded picture can be drawn by the previous drawing program. To make things simpler, we'll assume that there there will never be two consecutive occurrences of subpicture in a picture, i.e., (... subpicture subpicture ...) will never occur.

To make this useful, expand-picture must add the coordinates of the last point before the subpicture command to the coordinates of points in *insert* when they are inserted in the new picture. An example appears in Figure 15-2.

```
> (define complex
    '((move 100 100)
      subpicture
      (move 100 0)))
> (define simple
    '((draw 50 50)
      (draw 0 50)
      (draw 0 0)))
> (expand-picture complex simple)
((move 100 100)
 (draw 150 150)
 (draw 100 150)
 (draw 100 100)
 (move 100 0))
```

Figure 15-2   Expanding a picture

The picture simple was inserted in place of the symbol subpicture. But, before being inserted in the result, the coordinates of the commands in simple were increased by adding (100, 100) to them, the coordinates of the last point before the procedure.)

PROCEDURE (expand-picture *pic1 pic2*)

ARGUMENTS
- *pic1* is a list of picture commands, possibly containing subpicture
- *pic2* is a list of picture commands, without any occurrences of subpicture

RETURNS   a list of the picture commands in *pic1* where *pic2*, suitably translated, appears where subpicture appears in *pic1*

Design the procedure expand-picture according to this description. Make up a picture containing the symbol subpicture and a sub-picture. Expand the picture (show the resulting picture as a list of commands). Then plot the picture, the subpicture, and the expanded picture.

If you want to get even more adventurous, you could make expand-picture variadic. Instead of subpicture, the complex program contains integers that are replaced by the corresponding argument.

```
(expand-picture
  '((move 100 100) 2 (move 100 0) 1)
  ((draw 25 30))
  ((draw 50 100) (draw 50 50))) ⇒
((move 100 100) (draw 150 200) (draw 150 150)
 (move 100 0) (draw 125 30))
```

Deliverables: a listing of expand-picture and a printout showing that it works

Lab 16

A Blackjack Player

State is an important aspect of most games. If we are to write a computer program that plays a game, we must determine what state is needed, how to represent it, and how the state changes over time. A simple card game such as Blackjack gives us an opportunity to explore these concepts.

WHAT YOU NEED TO KNOW

Read the text through the end of Section 5.2. Make sure you understand boxes.

PROBLEM STATEMENT

In the game of Blackjack, a player attempts to get a score as close to 21 without going over. The rules are as follows:[1]
- A player is dealt two cards face down (only the player knows the cards).
- The player computes a score from the hand. Our simplified scoring method assigns 1 to aces, 2 through 10 for the number cards, and 10 to the jack, queen, and king; the suit doesn't matter.
- The player decides whether to ask for another card (the player says "hit me"). If so, the card is dealt face up.
- The process continues until either the player "stands" (at which point the player's cards are shown face up), or until the player's score goes over 21. The player who has the highest score that is not over 21 wins.

Normally, hands are dealt from the same deck, until the deck is exhausted.

In this lab, you will develop a Blackjack playing system. Your program will simulate the dealer and a player. The user is a second player. The program will deal cards to its own player; the user then has a chance to either be "hit" or to stand. There will be no betting in our version; the program will merely keep track of the number of hands won by either player.

In designing this program, you will need three abstract data types:
- card, representing a single card
- deck, representing the deck of up to 52 cards (some may already have been dealt)
- hand, representing the cards in a player's hand

Both hand and deck are represented as a list of cards, but the operations on a hand are different from those on a deck.

The two primary deck operations are shuffling a deck and dealing a card. If we imagine that a deck is only played once (a common casino practice), the constructor make-deck can shuffle the cards. A mutator deck-deal can deliver the next card to the player.

The hand operations are quite different: a new hand (delivered by the constructor make-hand) will be empty. We will need to know the score for a hand (an accessor); to add a card to the hand (a mutator); and to display the hand.

Even though the operations are different, the two ADTs can both be implemented as lists of cards. However, each list changes over time. One possibility is to use the set! form discussed in Section 5.3, and

---

[1] We have simplified the game in a number of ways from the version played in casinos. In the casino version, one card is face-up. In our version, face-up or -down doesn't matter. Also, in casinos the dealer is a player. Our dealer merely distributes cards, and doesn't actually play the game.

assign each of these lists to a global variable. However, this approach directly conflicts with data abstraction, and gets very tangled when we have more than one player. A much better way is to hide the state inside the ADTs, by storing the lists in boxes. We can freely mutate these boxes to add and delete cards.

The best general choice for the player is to stand on a score of 17 or higher, and to ask for another card for a lower score.

BEFORE THE LAB

1. Sketch out an interaction between the user and the computer while playing the game. What commands does the user type in? What are the computer responses?
2. Produce the ADT specifications (no code) for the three data types. Make sure you have specified all of the operations needed to deal cards, add cards to a hand, get a hand's score, and display a player's cards.
3. Write a module containing a procedure that plays the game, assuming the existence of the three ADTs. This procedure will create a deck and two hands. A helper procedure will simulate the computer player, and another one will interact with the user.
4. Implement the three ADTs you have specified, each in its own module.
5. Write three test drivers, one for each of the ADTs.

PITFALLS AND ADVICE

1. Make sure that your dealing is honest! You want to make sure that every card is dealt exactly once. This means that simply generating fifty-two random numbers between 1 and 52 won't work. The simplest method of making this work is to reject cards that have already been dealt, and to continue generating random cards until you have a complete deck.
2. If you have been reading ahead, or have experience with other programming languages, you might be tempted to use global variables. Don't! It will complicate your program.

CHECKPOINT

1. Draw a box-and-arrow diagram of a hand with three cards in it, showing how a fourth card is added.
2. If we want to rearrange the elements in a list randomly, we could write a (switch thelist 1st 2nd) procedure that switches the elements at positions 1st and 2nd. Write switch.
3. Joel starts with a variable thelist defined as () and wants to build a list by using set-car! or set-cdr! operations. Will this work?

DURING THE LAB

1. Type in your card ADT and its test driver, and make sure the ADT works. Put the printout showing this aside.
2. Type in your deck ADT and its test driver, and make sure the ADT works. Pay particular attention to showing that it is dealing fairly and honestly. Generate a printout.
3. Type in your hand ADT and its test driver, and produce a printout showing that it is correct.
4. Type in your game-playing module, and produce a printout showing that it works correctly.

AFTER THE LAB

1. Is it possible that your code for dealing cards could go into an infinite loop? Under what circumstances would this happen? Are you worried about this problem? What would you do to fix it?
2. Explain what you would do to modify the program so that there are more human and more computer players. (You don't need to write code.)
3. What happens when the program runs out of cards? How should you fix this?

DELIVERABLES

1. listings of the code for your program, and the printouts from "During the Lab"
2. your answers to the "After the Lab" questions

FOR FURTHER INVESTIGATION

Find out the complete set of casino rules, and modify your program to implement them. Casinos generally shuffle two decks together (giving a total of 104 cards).

Deliverables: a program listing and printout

Lab 17
Turtles

The purpose of this lab is to introduce the use of state in computing, leading to an object-oriented style of programming.

WHAT YOU NEED TO KNOW

Read up through Section 5.4 of the text. Make sure you understand procedures with state.

PROBLEM STATEMENT

In the late 1960s, researchers at Bolt Beranek and Newman, Inc., and MIT developed a robot called a "turtle." The original turtle was a small device that could move around the room, and could turn left or right. Soon, the turtle was equipped with a pen it could raise or lower, at which point it could draw pictures on a piece of paper placed on the floor. Legend has it that the turtle was so named because it was very slow when it worked, which was not much of the time.

One of the first programming languages that was given the power to control the turtle was Logo[1]. Logo's turtle is controlled by the commands

- forward *n*
  move the turtle *n* units in the direction in which it is facing.
- left *d*
  rotate the turtle left *d* degrees, without moving from its current position.
- penup
  raise the pen (i.e., future forward operations will not cause any mark to be left behind).
- pendown
  lower the pen (i.e., future forward operations will cause a line to be drawn).
- home
  put the turtle in the centre of the screen, with heading 0, and pen up.
- clearscreen
  Erase the screen, and home the turtle.

(Logo also has backward and right procedures, with the obvious meanings.)

Soon, Logo's users demanded the ability to have (simulated) turtles on a display screen. This allowed people not to have to spread out butcher paper in order to get a drawing; in fact, it allowed simple figures to be drawn very easily. (This explains the clearscreen command.)

How does a "display turtle" work? The screen (or the drawing window, to be precise) is measured in rectangular (Cartesian) coordinates. The turtle, on the other hand, does its drawing starting not at some absolute origin, but, rather, at its current position. The turtle also "knows" its current heading, in degrees.

Since we want to implement, in Scheme, "turtle procedures" that act as the Logo commands, we can implement the turtle procedures using four variables:

- turtle-x and turtle-y are the coordinates of the turtle;
- turtle-heading is the direction in which the turtle is currently facing;

---

[1] Logo, Scheme, and Smalltalk all have similar roots in Lisp. You may have seen Logo's turtles before. There is much more to Logo than turtles, though; the language supports lists, symbols, recursion, treating programs as data, and many other advanced features. See the Programming Problems at the end of Chapter 7 (pp. 408–409) for more information on Logo.

- `turtle-pen` is a Boolean that tells us whether the pen is down.

The specification for `forward` is:

PROCEDURE (`forward` n)

ARGUMENTS
- n is the number of steps

EFFECT   moves the turtle to the position as given in the equations and draws a line if the pen is down

---

You should be able to write similar specifications for the other turtle procedures.

All of the turtle procedures except `forward` can be implemented by setting the corresponding turtle variable; `forward` requires that we work out a new current position, and move (or draw, if the pen is down) to that position. Let's assume that we want to go forward n units; let the turtle's current position be (x_0, y_0), the heading be θ, and the new position be (x_1, y_1). The new position is:

$$x_1 = x_0 + n * \cos\theta$$
$$y_1 = y_0 + n * \sin\theta$$

(Scheme's trigonometric procedures work in radians.) Figure 17-1 shows how the turtle moves forward n steps.

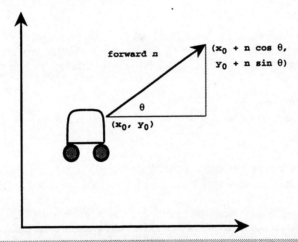

forward n

$(x_0 + n \cos\theta, \\ y_0 + n \sin\theta)$

θ

(x_0, y_0)

Figure 17-1   How the turtle moves

If you are implementing both `forward` and `backward`, you may want to have a helper procedure that does the actual drawing. Of course, you can implement them without a helper.

We can write a procedure to draw a square, using turtle graphics as in Program 17-1. One interesting class of turtle figures is the "polyspiral," whose definition is shown in Program 17-2.

It's possible to use `poly-spiral` to draw a circle. Figure out how to do this. (Hint: in a reasonably empty room, walk in a large circle. See what you do at each step.)

In this lab, you will build three implementations of turtles. The procedures to draw shapes with the turtle should not change with the different implementations.

```
(define square
  (lambda ()
    (forward 100)
    (right 90)
    (forward 100)
    (right 90)
    (forward 100)
    (right 90)
    (forward 100)
    (right 90)))
```

Program 17-1   Drawing a square

```
(define poly-spiral
  (lambda (nsteps fwd fwd-incr lf)
    (if (> nsteps 0)
      (begin
        (forward fwd)
        (left lf)
        (poly-spiral (sub1 nsteps) (+ fwd fwd-incr) fwd-incr lf)))))
```

Program 17-2   Polyspiral

Turtles with local variables

Our turtle has a bit of a problem: its variables are global, so that, by accident or on purpose, we can access them even without using the procedures. We are going to rewrite our turtle procedures to prevent this. The idea is that, instead of defining the turtle variables globally, we will bind them in a procedure:

```
(define turtle
  (let ((turtle-x 0) (turtle-y 0)
        (turtle-heading 0) (turtle-pen #f))
    (lambda ...
       ...)))
```

Unfortunately, the turtle variables are needed by *all* of the procedures, so we can't bind them in each one.[2] Obviously, if each of the turtle procedures has its own notion of where the turtle is, the turtle will not behave sensibly on the screen.

It's easy to fix this, though: let's just write *one* procedure as in Program 17-3.

```
(define turtle
  (let ((turtle-x 0) (turtle-y 0)
        (turtle-heading 0) (turtle-pen #f))
    (lambda (what . args)
      (if (eqv? what 'forward)
          (begin ... do whatever we need to to move
                     forward )
          (if (eqv? what 'left)
              (begin ... do whatever we need to turn
                         left )
              (if (eqv? what 'penup)
                  ... and so on))))))
```

Program 17-3   A turtle procedure with state

---

[2] By the rules of lexical scoping, if we bound them separately in each procedure, we would have separate variables.

PROCEDURE (turtle *what . args*)

ARGUMENTS
- *what* is a symbol that denotes the turtle operation
- *args* is bound to the list of remaining arguments that say how far forward, or how many degrees left, the turtle moves

EFFECT   changes the turtle's pen or orientation, or moves the turtle

To move the turtle forward, we say

```
(turtle 'forward 50)
```

and to raise the pen, we say

```
(turtle 'penup)
```

We can make this a bit nicer by defining procedures such as

```
(define forward
  (lambda (n) (turtle 'forward n)))
(define penup
  (lambda () (turtle 'penup)))
```

More than one turtle

It is possible to have a number of turtles, each with its own position, heading, and pen state. To explore this, we're going to build yet a third turtle implementation. The template for this procedure, called make-turtle, appears in Program 17-4.

```
(define make-turtle
  (lambda ()
    (let ((turtle-x 0) ...)
      (lambda (what . args)
        (if (eqv? what 'forward)
          ...)))))
```

Program 17-4   make-turtle

Now, when we call make-turtle, we get back a procedure that has its own turtle variables; this procedure has the same arguments as the procedure returned by turtle. For example,

```
(define joe (make-turtle))
(joe 'forward 50)
```

defines a turtle joe and moves joe forward 50 units.

Instead of (forward 50), we can use (joe 'forward 50) to move joe. The make-turtle procedure must be careful how to manage the pen for multiple turtles, since there's only one (x, y) coordinate for the pen in the drawing package.

You need to finish off make-turtle and write a new forward that can move just one particular turtle forward by the specified amount, so that you can test all your turtle shape procedures with the same interface.

Turtles have very interesting behavior. In fact, a very simple turtle can describe some extremely complex mathematical and physical systems. Harold Abelson and Andy diSessa wrote a book, *Turtle Geometry*, in which they explored these ideas. (Warning: the book is full of heavy-duty math.)

In this lab, you are building three implementations of turtles. Your square, triangle, and plus sign procedures should have work unchanged with the different implementations. This is a result of abstraction: because the details of how the turtle is implemented are hidden inside procedures, we can change those details without changing the procedures that use the turtle. In Chapter 6, you will see that what we've done is in fact a kind of object-oriented programming.

BEFORE THE LAB

1. Write a set of turtle procedures as described above. You will use the global variables described above (turtle-x and friends), and use set! to change them.[3] Many of your procedures will be defined with no parameters:

```
(define penup
  (lambda ()
    ... raise the pen ...))
```

and so on.

2. Prepare procedures like square that use the turtle to draw a triangle and a plus sign, respectively.
3. Design the turtle procedure.
4. Design the make-turtle procedure.

CHECKPOINT

1. Write a form that draw a hexagon, using poly-spiral.
2. turtle needs to keep local state. If you understand how turtle does this, you should be able to explain why this "collector" doesn't seem to keep the elements it has been given.

```
(define collector
  (lambda args
    (let ((collection '()))
      (if (eqv? (car args) 'put)
        (set! collection (cons (car (cdr args)) collection))
        collection))))
```

3. In the turtle procedure, the *x* and *y* values are not stored in global variables. Where are they stored?

DURING THE LAB

1. Create a module with your turtle procedures, and test them out, using the square, triangle, and plus sign procedures you have written (these should not be in the module). Save your code in turtle.scm.
2. Experiment with the following:
   - (poly-spiral 100 100 0 90)
   - (poly-spiral 100 50 1 90)
   - (poly-spiral 100 50 0 89)
   - (poly-spiral 100 50 1 121)
3. Use poly-spiral to draw a circle.
4. Create a module with your revised turtle procedure (the one that uses local variables) in file turt-loc.scm. Test it with your square, triangle, and plus sign procedures.
5. Create another revised module with your make-turtle procedure (that lets us have multiple turtles) in file turtmult.scm. Test it with your square, triangle, and plus sign procedures.

AFTER THE LAB

The approach taken in this lab is called "encapsulation." We wanted to prevent outside code from accessing the internal state of a turtle; we used a technique sometimes called "let-over-lambda," in which the let establishes bindings that last from one call of the procedure to the next, to remember that state.

This brings up an interesting question: why did we have to use turtle? Why not use let-over-lambda to hide the variables in each procedure, e.g.,

---

[3] Because of the use of set!, these will be mutant turtles.

```
(define forward
  (let ((turtle-x ...
    (lambda (n) ...
(define left
  (let ((turtle-x ...
    (lambda (n) ...
```

Use the environment model to provide an answer to this question. Draw the snapshots for both `turtle` and the version of `forward` and `left` shown here; using these snapshots, show why we have to use `turtle`.

Turtle procedures resemble, in a way, the `subpicture` command in the picture language. How?

DELIVERABLES

1. your turtle procedures (from `turtle.scm`) and your tests (plots) using the square, triangle, and plus sign procedures you have written

2. your experiments with the poly-spiral

3. a listing of the form that uses a polyspiral to draw a circle

4. your second turtle package (from `turtlep.scm`) and your tests (plots) using the square, triangle, and plus sign procedures you have written

5. listings of your `make-turtle` procedure (from `turtleo.scm`) and the new procedure that moves a turtle forward

6. your snapshots from the "After the Lab" part and your answers to the questions

Be sure you identify what output came from which program. Don't hand in repeated code.

FOR FURTHER INVESTIGATION

Another possibility is to have a **brigade**, a list of turtles that all follow the same rules. For example

```
(define joe (make-turtle))
(define mary (make-turtle))
(define lee (make-turtle))
(define jml (make-brigade (list joe mary lee)))
(jml 'forward 10)
```

The last form causes each turtle in the brigade to move forward 10 units.

Of course, the `jml` brigade as it is isn't terribly useful. The problem is that all three of the turtles start off with the same internal state (position and heading). This isn't a problem: you can rewrite `make-turtle` to accept an initial position and direction for a turtle, so you can start each of the turtles in the brigade off at a different place, we can end up with a complex drawing made up of the same part repeated in many different places.

Sending a message to a brigade is actually very simple: we just use `for-each` to send the message to each turtle in the brigade. Use the same technique as in `make-turtle` to remember the list of turtles in the brigade.

Write a module that implements brigades.

Deliverables: a listing of the new `make-turtle` and a printout showing that brigades work

Lab 18

Adventures in Objectland

Object-oriented programming is mostly useful for "programming-in-the-large". A large program is too complicated for a person to be able to keep all the details in mind; larger programs also require ongoing extension and maintenance. Most large problems are about people or things in the real world. Object-oriented programming helps us because it concentrates upon the **entities** in the problem and how they interact.

In this and the next lab we will explore two key ideas: the simulation of a world in which objects are characterized by a set of state variables, and the use of objects and classes as a programming technique for modularizing worlds in which objects interact. We'll also learn some techniques for understanding large blocks of code.

WHAT YOU NEED TO KNOW

Read up to the end of Section 6.2. Make sure you understand the `define-class` form.

PROBLEM STATEMENT

One of the earliest computer games was known as "Adventure". In this game, a human player explores a world that contains interesting places and objects. The Adventure world includes various magical beings, some of whom are not very friendly. Adventure games have become quite popular; the Zork games are a well-known version.

The user plays the game by issuing commands that have the effect of moving him or her around in the imaginary world, or performing acts such as picking up an object. The computer simulates the player's moves and responds to them, allowing legal moves and rejecting illegal ones. For example, it is illegal to move between places that are not connected (unless you have a magic wand). If a move is legal, the computer updates its model of the world and allows the next move to be considered.

Adventure is an ideal application for object-oriented programming. The player, the beings the player interacts with, the places the player visits, and the things the player encounters can all be represented as objects. Sometimes these objects interact. For example, the player might walk into a room in which another being is already present. This other being, noticing that a new person has entered the room, says, "Hello". All of this behavior can be implemented by ensuring that the various objects send each other messages to indicate what is happening.

The authors have built the framework for a basic Adventure game; it is found in the goodie advent.scm. We've defined the classes `person`, `place`, and `thing`. It will be your job in this lab and the next to use these classes to build a simple world. Rather than dealing with magical monsters, our world will be a college campus, inhabited by faculty members, deans, and maybe the occasional troll. Figure 18-1 shows the world our creatures will inhabit.

Pieces of The Game

After loading the goodie, we can create two faculty members, and seeing how they move around in the world.

```
> (define jim (make-person 'jim jim-office 1))
> (define vincent (make-person 'vincent vincent-office 2))
```

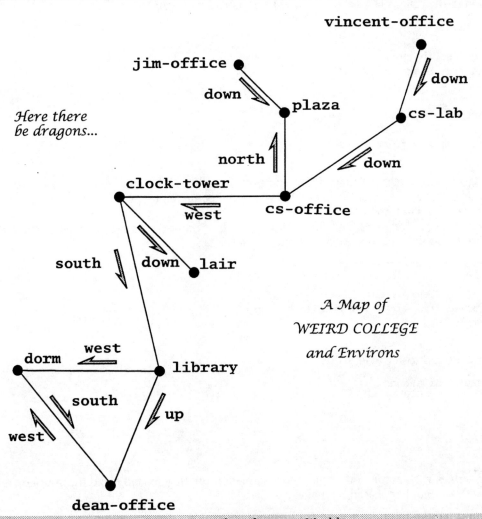

Figure 18-1   The Adventure World

persons have three attributes: their name, their original location, and a "restlessness threshold", which we'll explain later. jim-office and vincent-office are instances of class place; they're defined, along with a large number of other places, in the goodie. Each place has a large number of exits to other places.

Jim decides to go for a walk:

```
> (jim 'current-position)
jim-office
> (jim 'exits)
(down)
> (jim 'go 'down)
jim moved from jim-office to plaza.
moved
> (jim 'current-position)
plaza
```

He discovers he's in his office; he notices that the only exit leads downwards (perhaps via a trap-door; the Computer Science building was designed by a firm of deranged architects), and finds himself in the plaza outside the Student Union.

Jim is an **object** in the sense that he responds to messages. Three messages were sent to him in this example: current-position, exits and go *direction*. As in the book, each message consists of a symbol that selects a method in the object jim, followed by zero or more arguments.

```
> (jim 'exits)
(up south)
> (jim 'go 'south)
jim moved from plaza to cs-office.
moved
> (jim 'exits)
(west north up)
> (jim 'go 'up)
jim moved from cs-office to cs-lab.
moved
```

Each command to jim produces a return value: exits returns a list of the directions from which he can leave the current place; go always returns the symbol moved. Some commands also have an effect: go also displays a message saying where jim moves from and to.

Jim does a bit more traveling, and finds himself in the Computer Science Lab. Meanwhile, Vincent is getting a bit bored, and decides to see what's going on in the lab.

```
> (vincent 'current-position)
vincent-office
> (vincent 'go 'down)
vincent moved from vincent-office to cs-lab.
vincent says: Hi, jim.
moved
```

Both people look around to see what's there.

```
> (vincent 'look-around)
jim
ok
> (jim 'look-around)
vincent
ok
```

A courier arrives with some new computer documentation. (If you don't like the courier explanation, you can assume the manual appeared by magic.)

```
> (define scheme-manual (make-thing 'scheme-manual))
> (cs-lab 'appear scheme-manual)
appeared
```

Jim notices the manual first, picks it up, and leaves before Vincent notices. Because Jim took it, the manual travels with him.

```
> (jim 'look-around)
scheme-manual
vincent
ok
> (jim 'take scheme-manual)
jim took scheme-manual
taken
> (jim 'list-possessions)
scheme-manual
ok
> (jim 'go 'down)
jim moved from cs-lab to cs-office.
moved
> (jim 'list-possessions)
scheme-manual
ok
```

Vincent finally realizes Jim took the manual. He follows Jim, and in a titanic struggle he takes the manual away from Jim.[1]

```
> (vincent 'go 'down)
vincent moved from cs-lab to cs-office.
vincent says: Hi, jim.
moved
> (vincent 'take scheme-manual)
vincent took scheme-manual
Yaaaah! jim is upset!
taken
> (vincent 'list-possessions)
scheme-manual
ok
> (jim 'list-possessions)
ok
```

Vincent has the manual, and Jim no longer does. A message to Vincent must have resulted in Jim being sent a second message advising him that he no longer has the manual.

The Ticking Clock

In principle, we could run the Adventure system by simply issuing commands to each of the creatures in the world, as we did above. This, however, defeats the notion of the game, since the user has control over all the creatures. Instead, we will structure our system so that all the characters, with the possible exception of ourselves, are manipulated in some fashion by the computer, while we are able only to control our own actions.

Therefore, we will create a collection of all the creatures currently active in our world. We will also have a simulated clock that keeps track of time. Each time the clock "ticks", a `clock-tick` message is sent to each of the creatures. We will define for each kind of creature how it responds to a tick. `persons` respond by moving, but only if their restlessness has reached the threshold given as the third argument to `make-person`. Since different people get bored at different rates, this argument is different for each `person` in the world. A `person`'s restlessness value is increased by 1 on each clock tick.

To see how the clock works, we reloaded the code (so that Jim and Vincent are back in their offices, with no Scheme manual in existence), and called `demo-clock`, a procedure that runs the clock for n ticks.

```
> (define demo-clock
    (lambda (n)
      (if (> n 0)
        (begin
          (clock)
          (format #t "Tick!~%")
          (demo-clock (- n 1))))))
> (demo-clock 10)
Tick!
jim moved from jim-office to plaza.
Tick!
vincent moved from vincent-office to cs-lab.
Tick!
jim moved from plaza to cs-office.
Tick!
Tick!
vincent moved from cs-lab to cs-office.
vincent says: Hi, jim.
jim moved from cs-office to plaza.
Tick!
```

---

[1] Lest anyone get the wrong idea, the authors of this Lab Manual are good friends, and would never fight over anything as insignificant as a manual.

```
Tick!
jim moved from plaza to jim-office.
Tick!
vincent moved from cs-office to plaza.
Tick!
jim moved from jim-office to plaza.
jim says: Hi, vincent.
Tick!
```

Because we haven't made our creatures very interesting (they *are* faculty members, after all), the automated Adventure isn't that interesting: the creatures wander aimlessly. Creatures do have behavior, though: when a creature enters a place that's already inhabited, it greets the creature that was already there. We can make much more interesting creatures: a student in possession of late homework might attempt to force any faculty member it encounters to accept the late homework. When you have completed this and the next lab, you will know enough to make the Adventure world and its creatures as interesting as you like.

Defining the Classes

How do we define the various creatures, places, and things of our world? Each is defined as a class that responds to a set of messages. The simplest of these is the class thing, shown in Program 18-1; we will look at this class here, and leave the classes person and place to the next lab. A thing has one constructor argument, the symbol that names it. The only instance variable is the identity of the current possessor of the thing. The methods are:

- type returns the symbol thing. Each class (person, place, and thing) must implement type; there are times when the program must be able to tell what sort of entity it is handling.

- name is an accessor.

- change-possessor and possessor allow us to identify and mutate the identity of the thing's possessor.

- Each time clock is called, it sends a clock-tick message to each person, place, and thing. Each class must have a corresponding method. Since things don't have any spontaneous behavior, the method shown here is a no-operation.

- By default, define-class adds an else clause that generates a fatal error. There are times when users type in messages to objects (as in our top-level, shown below). Therefore, we include an else clause that displays an error message, but doesn't cause an actual Scheme error.

```
(define-class thing
  (constructor-arguments name)
  (slots (possessor 'no-one))
  (methods (mess . args)
    ((type) 'thing)
    ((name)  name)
    ((change-possessor)
      (set! possessor (car args)))
    ((clock-tick) "Nothing to do.")
    ((possessor) possessor)
    (else
      (format #t
        "~a didn't understand the command ~a.~%"
        name mess))))
(define make-thing
  (lambda (name)
    (let ((a (thing 'make name)))
      (add-object a)
      a)))
```

Program 18-1   The thing class

We create objects not by sending a make message to the class, but by calling a separate procedure named make-*class*, e.g., make-person to create a new person. We chose this technique because many objects must not only be created but also initialized in various ways. A limitation of define-class is that we can't attach additional code to the built-in make method. We could require that we send each object an initialize message first, but this is clumsy and error-prone.

PROCEDURE (make-thing *name*)

ARGUMENTS
  • *name* is a symbol that is the thing's name.

RETURNS   the newly created thing.

PROCEDURE (make-place *name*)

ARGUMENTS
  • *name* is a symbol that is the place's name.

RETURNS   the newly created place.

---

places are connected by calling can-go.

PROCEDURE (can-go *place1 direction place2*)

ARGUMENTS
  • *place1* is a place from which creatures can travel.
  • *direction* is a symbol naming a direction.
  • *place2* is the place located in the specified direction.

EFFECT   modifies the game's data structures so that place1 and place2 are connected.

PROCEDURE (make-person *name place threshold*)

ARGUMENTS
  • *name* is a symbol that is the person's name.
  • *place* is a place (*not* a symbol that is the place's name) in which the person is initially located.
  • *threshold* is an integer that says how many clock ticks will elapse before the person gets bored and decides to move somewhere. Lower values make persons more restless.

RETURNS   the newly-created person.

We have already described the messages sent to things. The messages sent to persons and places will be described in detail in the next lab. The messages a player might send to persons are:
  • look-around: display every object at the same place as the person.
  • take *thing*: obtain possession of the *thing*, whether or not somebody else owns it.
  • list-possessions: display all the possessions owned by the person.
  • current-position: return the name of the place at which the person is located.
  • exits: return a list of the directions in which the person can move from the current place.
  • go *direction*: go to the place in the specified direction.

Any game must have a player. Our player will be a person named player, with an extremely high restlessness threshold. Normally, the player in the computer moves only in response to commands from the human player. (Lowering the restlessness threshold would mean that the player would periodically move on its own.)

The final stage is to build a "top-level" for the world. This top-level will create a player object, and will allow the human player to type in commands to the player. After each command, the clock procedure is run. The prompt ?? asks the player for a command; the resulting value of the command is prefixed with ==.

```
> (adventure)
Welcome to Weird College Adventure!
You were working all night trying to finish your computer
science lab. Finally you fell asleep at your computer.
You awake, remembering nothing except that you must get
the assignment handed in to your instructor immediately.

Your initial location is plaza.
?? (exits)
== (up south)
?? (go up)
player moved from plaza to jim-office.
player says: Hi, jim.
== moved
jim moved from jim-office to plaza.
?? (exits)
== (down)
vincent moved from vincent-office to cs-lab.
?? (go down)
player moved from jim-office to plaza.
player says: Hi, jim.
== moved
jim moved from plaza to cs-office.
?? quit
bye
```

A command to the top-level is given in parentheses. It consists of a message to send, along with the arguments needed. The command `quit` (a symbol, not a list) exits from the top-level.

The biggest obstacle in building the top level is handling inputs that are are *data*, not program code. Suppose the user enters (take scheme-manual). How is the program to know that the symbol `scheme-manual` means the value of the variable `scheme-manual`?

We must follow two rules to solve this problem:

1. The name of each person, place, or thing must be the same as the name of the variable to which it is assigned, e.g.,

   ```
   (define jim (make-person 'jim jim-office 1))
   ```

2. We must keep an association list that allows us to translate a symbol into the corresponding value.

The best way to manage this is to ensure that when an object is created it is placed on the translation list. When the top level needs to translate the name of an object into the object itself, it calls `translate-name-to-object`, shown in Program 18-2. In this code, `all-objects` is the list of objects managed by the clock.

Directions are placed on the initial translation list. When a `person`, `place`, or `thing` is created, its name and value are placed on the translation list. For example, if we do

   ```
   > (define scheme-manual (make-thing 'scheme-manual))
   ```

the pair (scheme-manual . <scheme-manual object>) is placed on the translation list. (It is often convenient for a constructor to do more than just initialize the instance variables; in this case, we are also inserting the object into a data structure. It would be possible to write a class method that creates the object and inserts it onto the translation list. We prefer to create a procedure such as `make-thing` that does this.)

We have to be careful about translating, because people are typing in the commands that are translated. `translate-name-to-object` returns either the value or #f if the name isn't known. The best strategy is to translate the cdr of the command; if #f is found in the resulting list, then the entire command is rejected.

The car of a command is not translated. It is the command that is sent to the player. It is therefore essential that the class `person` have an `else` clause, rather than relying on the default, which is to cause a fatal program error.

```
(define all-objects '())

(define translations '(
  (north . north)
  (south . south)
  (east . east)
  (west . west)
  (up . up)
  (down . down)
))

(define add-object
  (lambda (object)
    (set! all-objects (cons object all-objects))
    (set! translations
      (cons
        (cons (object 'name) object)
        translations))
    'added))

(define clock
  (lambda ()
    (for-each
      (lambda (x)
        (if (not (eqv? x player)) (x 'clock-tick)))
      all-objects)))

(define translate-name-to-object
  (lambda (sym)
    (let ((x (assv sym translations)))
      (if x
        (cdr x)
        (begin
          (format #t "I don't know ~a.~%" sym)
          #f)))))
```

Program 18-2   Managing Objects

An example of a less-than-successful session that uses this error-handling is

```
> (adventure)
Welcome to Weird College Adventure!

You awake, remembering nothing except that you must
get an assignment handed in to your instructor
immediately. Your initial location is plaza.
?? (go northeast)
I don't know northeast.
I couldn't follow your instructions.
?? (duh)
player didn't understand the command duh.
== #t
?? quit
bye
```

The people, places, and things in our world have many other features built in, and it is recommended that you look carefully at the code to see some of them. Still other features could readily be added; building such programs is often a good deal of fun. For the rest of this laboratory, we'll concentrate on a few aspects of the world we have built.

BEFORE THE LAB

Most of the work in this lab needs to be done at the computer. Therefore most of your pre-lab work will be to read the above problem description carefully and to make sure you understand it.

1. Write a set of can-go calls corresponding to the map in Figure 18-1.

2. Examine the code for the class thing. Write the definition of a new class, meltable-thing, that melts after a given number of clock ticks.

   ```
   > (define ice-cream-bar
       (make-meltable-thing ice-cream-bar 2))
   > (clock-tower 'appear ice-cream-bar)
   appeared
   > (clock)
   > (clock)
   ice-cream-bar melted.
   ```

PITFALLS AND ADVICE

1. Study the code and this lab carefully before you attempt to solve any of the problems. The hard part of the lab is understanding the object-oriented framework, not writing the code once you understand the framework.

2. The best way to proceed is to create your own file in which you place your own code. Each time you try something, load the goodie and your file into Scheme (reloading the goodie ensures that the game can be reinitialized properly). One convenient way to do all of this is to create a third file containing nothing but two calls to load, one to load each of the files. Your Scheme system may have another way to reload a package of files conveniently: ask your instructor. You might be tempted to make a copy of the goodie, and put your changes directly into the copy. This is not a good idea, because it will be hard for you to see what code you wrote, and what code was part of the goodie.

CHECKPOINT

1. In the dialog

   ```
   > (vincent 'take scheme-manual)
   vincent took scheme-manual
   Yaaaah! jim is upset!
   taken
   ```

   what state changes occur, and to what objects?

2. Why do we have to have translations (i.e., why can't we just apply the player object to the list of symbols read in for a command)?

3. In the Adventure world, if you can go from place A to place B, does the way we represent the world necessarily allow you to go from B to A? Why or why not?

DURING THE LAB

1. Make jim and vincent move around by repeatedly calling clock (with no arguments). Which person is more restless? How often do both of them move at the same time?

2. Create a thing called late-homework, and put it in the plaza. Put yourself in the plaza. Pick up the late-homework, find out where jim is using the message current-position, and move yourself to jim's location. Try to get jim to take the homework even though it's late. Can you find a way to do this that does not leave you upset?

3. Type in your meltable-thing class and get it to work.

AFTER THE LAB

1. Suppose we evaluate

   ```
   > (define floppy-disk (make-thing 'floppy-disk))
   > (floppy-disk 'type)
   ```

   Referring to Program 18-1, draw a snapshot of the frames and procedures that are created during the evaluation.

2. Each time the clock ticks, objects get `clock-tick` messages. Does it make any difference in what order the objects receive their tick messages? Why or why not?

DELIVERABLES

1. transcripts of your sessions
2. a listing of your `meltable-thing` class
3. answers to your "After the Lab" questions

Lab 19
Further Adventures in Objectland

Object-oriented programs can be extended in many ways. New messages can be added, and new classes that understand existing messages can be defined. We can see how this is possible by extending our Adventure game to support entirely new kinds of creatures.

WHAT YOU NEED TO KNOW

This lab depends on the material up to the end of Section 6.2. You must have completed Lab 18 before you start work on this lab.

PROBLEM STATEMENT

In this lab, you'll add more creatures to the Adventure world. Each kind of creature will be represented as a class.

The Luddite[1] Dean

First is an officious Dean who hates computers. The Dean is quite restless, and wanders about the campus; any time he encounters someone who has a computer, the Dean takes it and smashes it. A typical dialog goes something like this:

```
?? (current-position)
plaza
?? (look-around)
computer
==ok
?? (take computer)
taken
?? (list-possessions)
computer
==ok
Dean Snerd moved from cs-office to plaza.
Dean Snerd says -- Aha! I see you have a computer with you!
Dean Snerd says -- I will smash it!
Dean Snerd moved from plaza to dean-office.
?? (list-possessions)
== ok
```

In this example, the player was in the plaza. Seeing a computer, the player picked it up, only to blunder into Dean Snerd, who had just wandered into the plaza. The dean smashes the computer (list-possessions shows that the player no longer has it), and then magically transports himself back to the Deanery (there, no doubt,

---

[1] British textile workers in the early nineteenth century were often afraid—with good reason—that their jobs would vanish as more machinery was installed. They began destroying the machinery. As they claimed to be followers of a possibly fictitious Ned Lud or Ludd, they were often called Luddites. In modern usage, a Luddite is a person who strongly doubts that technology contributes to human happiness.

to sulk about technology).[2] For the purposes of this lab, a computer is any `thing` whose name is `computer`. All computers are the same to the program (as they are to Dean Snerd).

`deans` have one magic power: wherever a dean may be on the college campus, it can transport itself back to its office any time it smashes a computer.

An encounter with a dean need not result in a smashed computer. A dean has a `officiousness` value, which is incremented by 1 on each move. The computer is smashed only if this value is greater than the dean's officiousness threshold; this threshold is specified when the dean is created. A dialog with a not-very-officious dean might look like:

```
?? (current-position)
plaza
?? (look-around)
computer
==ok
?? (take computer)
taken
?? (list-possessions)
computer
==ok
Dean Snerd moved from cs-office to plaza.
Dean Snerd says -- Aha! I see you have a computer with you!
Dean Snerd says -- I'm not in the mood to smash it this time,
but don't let me see it next time!
Dean Snerd moved from plaza to dean-office.
?? (list-possessions)
computer
== ok
```

A dean's officiousness threshold doesn't affect its desire to wander the campus. After two clock ticks, the dean will leave its office and wander the campus.

The Pizza-Eating Troll

Our next creature is a `troll` named Grendel, who normally lives in a lair concealed under the `clock-tower`. `trolls` have quite simple needs. Normally they sit in their lairs; after a certain number of clock intervals, they get hungry and leave the lair to wander around the world seeking food. A `troll` will eat the first person it runs into, unless that person can offer it the one food all `trolls` like better: pizza. When a troll finishes eating, it returns to its lair.

Suppose some poor soul named `tommy` is in the Main Library when `grendel`, comes along.

```
> (tommy 'current-position)
main-lib
> (grendel 'move)
grendel moved from clock-tower to main-lib
grendel says -- Hssss--s!  I'm going to eat you, tommy!!
grendel says -- Grovel, you low-on-the-food-chain human!
tommy grovels.
grendel eats tommy and belches.
grendel moved from main-lib to dungeon
moved
> (tommy 'current-position)
heaven
```

We've directly manipulated `tommy` and `grendel` in this example, rather than using the top-level. We did this because the interactions between `persons` and `trolls` are fairly intricate, and we didn't want clock ticks, and the behavior they trigger, to confuse matters.

---

[2] We have made our Dean nasty for dramatic effect only. The Deans we have met over the years have uniformly been fine people who would never dream of smashing computers that didn't belong to them.

On the other hand, if `tommy` had been carrying a `pizza`, the incident above would have had a happier ending:

```
> (tommy 'current-position)
main-lib
> (tommy 'list-possessions)
pizza
> (grendel 'move)
grendel moved from clock-tower to main-lib
grendel says  --  Hssss--s!  I'm going to eat you, tommy!!
grendel says  --  Grovel, you low-on-the-food-chain human!
tommy grovels.
tommy says  --  Take this pizza instead, please!
grendel says  --  OK, thanks for not putting any anchovies on it!
grendel moved from main-lib to dungeon
moved
> (tommy 'list-possessions)
```

`grendel`'s behavior suggests that the player always keep a pizza at hand. This is a bit of a problem, because we don't have anywhere to get pizza (a problem that many students trying to finish off labs late at night have encountered). We must therefore add a Pizzeria to the campus. A player who goes to the Pizzeria may find a pizza available for pickup. If not, the player must wait for two moves for Luigi, the proprietor, to bake one. (Luigi never leaves the Pizzeria.)

```
?? current-position
pizzeria
?? look-around
== ok
?? look-around
luigi says -- Your pizza is available for pickup.
?? look-around
pizza
== ok
```

Even with Luigi's excellent pizzas, the troll seems to have a distinct advantage (rumors that the troll is a slightly demented former Computer Science instructor are apparently unfounded). We can even things up a bit in the following manner. The default `grovel` method for `persons` merely displays a message. We can modify this method so that groveling results in a 25% chance that the `person` will be magically transported to a nearby place, selected at random from the places one can reach from the current position. Groveling is not without risk: there is also a 25% chance that the `person` will be expelled from the College (or, worse, be forced to take a Cobol course). There is also a 50% chance that nothing will happen at all. Trolls only attempt to eat people at the same place they are in. A transported person is in a different place when the troll attempts to dine, and an expelled person is in (Cobol) heaven. In either case, the `troll`'s appetite will remain unsatisfied.

```
?? current-position
== library
?? grovel
?? current-position
== library
?? grovel
You have violated Section 4.3.2.8.55.22 of the Student
Code. You are therefore expelled, and the game is over.
```

The Magic Wand

Many Adventure games include rods, staffs, and wands that have magical properties such as teleportation. We will create a magic wand, powered by a small battery, and containing an embedded microprocessor running a Scheme program. Waving a wand results in a magical transfer to one of the places adjacent to the current position. Wands contain a certain number of charges, one of which is expended when it is waved. Waving an uncharged wand has no effect. There is only one wand-recharger on campus, in the computer lab. This recharger gives two charges.

A Trip Around Campus

We now have enough people, places, and things to build a complete game. Your goal is to get from the dorm to the computer-store, pick up a computer, and then go to the pizzeria for a pizza, and get back to the dorm for an all-night debugging session without losing your possessions or being eaten by any trolls. (You will have to add the computer store to the set of campus places.) You should stop at the computer-lab first to get the magic wand. Remember that in order to allow the other creatures in the world to interact, you must alternate your moves with calls to clock.

BEFORE THE LAB

1. Study the person class and the make-person procedure, shown in Programs 19-1, 19-2, and 19-3. Identify the changes you will need to make to class person in order to support the grovel message.
2. Write a dean class and a corresponding make-dean procedure, based upon person.
3. Build a troll class, with the behavior described above.
4. Study the thing class, presented in Lab 18, and use it as the basis for a wand class.
5. Write one test driver procedure for each of the classes you are building in this lab. The test driver should create the necessary objects, and put them through their paces, writing out the results.

PITFALLS AND ADVICE

T he person class makes use of a feature known as self. In a method in a define-class form, the variable self can be used. self is automatically bound to the current object. This feature has a number of uses, of which the most important are that one method can call a second method in the same class by doing (self 'another-method), and an object can ask another to do some work on its behalf by doing (another-object 'do-it self).

CHECKPOINT

1. What should happen if a dean meets a troll? Will the possession of computers or pizza change the outcome?
2. Who sends the grovel message?
3. What state variable or variables must the Pizzeria class have?

DURING THE LAB

1. Enter your modifications to person, and test that instances of this class respond to grovel properly.
2. Enter and test your dean implementation.
3. Enter your troll code, and test it out.
4. Enter your wand code, and test it out.
5. Make the necessary revisions to the top-level to support the new kinds of creatures and wands. The game should start in the dorm.
6. Play the game, tempting fate by walking past the clock tower (with or without pizza), and walking past the Dean's Office holding an extremely expensive notebook computer. You will have several sessions, in some of which you will lose, and in at least one of which you will arrive back at the dorm with your possessions intact. Make a transcript of your game sessions.

AFTER THE LAB

1. Review the code you wrote in this lab. How, if at all, did the division of code into classes help you? Write a brief report answering this question.

```
(define-class person
  (constructor-arguments name place threshold)
  (slots (possessions '()) (restlessness 0))
  (methods (mess . args)
    ((create) (place 'appear self))
    ((type) 'person)
    ((name) name)
    ((place) place)
    ((grovel) (format #t "~a grovels.~%" name))
    ((look-around)
      (for-each
        (lambda (thing)
          (if (not (eqv? self thing))
            (format #t "~a~%" (thing 'name))))
        (place 'things))
      'ok)
    ((take)
      (let ((thing (car args)))
        (if (thing? thing)
          (if (memv thing (place 'things))
            (begin
              (format #t "~a took ~a~%" name (thing 'name))
              (set! possessions (cons thing possessions))
              (for-each
                (lambda (p)
                  (if (and (not (eqv? p self))
                           (memv thing (p 'possessions)))
                    (begin
                      (p 'lose thing)
                      (have-fit p))))
                (filter person? (place 'things)))
              (thing 'change-possessor self)
              'taken)
            (fatal-error "Thing taken not at this place"
              (list (place 'name) (thing 'name))))
          (fatal-error "not a thing" (thing 'name)))))
    ((lose)
      (let ((thing (car args)))
        (set! possessions (delete thing possessions))
        (thing 'change-possessor 'no-one)
        'lost))
```

Program 19-1   The person class, Part 1 of 3

DELIVERABLES

1. code listings and test execution output for each of the classes
2. a transcript of your game sessions

```
    ((list-possessions)
      (for-each
        (lambda (thing)
          (format #t "~a~%" (thing 'name)))
        possessions)
      'ok)
    ((current-position)
      (place 'name))
    ((exits)
      (place 'exits))
    ((go)
      (let ((direction (car args)))
        (let ((new-place (place 'look-in direction)))
          (if (not (null? new-place))
            (self 'move-to new-place)
            (begin
              (format #t
                "~a can't go ~a from ~a.~%" name
                direction (place 'name))))))
      'moved)
    ((possessions) possessions)
    ((clock-tick)
      (set! restlessness (add1 restlessness))
      (if (> restlessness threshold)
        (let ((new-place (random-place place)))
      (if (not (null? new-place))
        (self 'move-to new-place)))))
    ((go-to-heaven)
      (for-each (lambda (p) (me 'lose p)) possessions)
      (place 'gone self)
      (heaven 'appear self)
      (set! place heaven)
      'dead)
```

Program 19-2   The person class, Part 2 of 3

```
    ((move-to)
      (let ((new-place (car args)))
        (announce-move name place new-place)
        (set! restlessness 0)
        (for-each
          (lambda (p)
            (place 'gone p)
            (new-place 'appear p))
          possessions)
        (let
          ((new-place-people
             (filter person? (new-place 'things))))
          (if (not (null? new-place-people))
            (begin
              (format #t "~a says: Hi," name)
              (for-each
                (lambda (p)
                  (format #t " ~a" (p 'name)))
                new-place-people)
              (format #t ".~%"))))
        (place 'gone self)
        (new-place 'appear self)
        (set! place new-place)))
      (else
        (format #t
          "~a didn't understand the command ~a.~%"
          name mess))))

(define make-person
  (lambda (name place threshold)
    (let ((a (person 'make name place threshold)))
      (a 'create)
      (add-object a)
      a)))
```

Program 19-3   The person class, Part 3 of 3

Lab 20

Computer Networks

Our main objectives in this lab are to familiarize you with object-oriented programming and acquaint you with the basic structure of computer networks. In this lab, we use objects to simulate a computer network that is an abstraction of real networks including Netware, TCP/IP, Lantastic, and IBM's LAN Server. All the features found here are in these real systems.

You will be given an implementation of the network. In Lab 21 you will be asked to extend the implementation in several ways. Objects can communicate with each other by sending messages and, sometimes, the objects themselves.

WHAT YOU NEED TO KNOW

Read up through Section 6.2. Make sure you understand how classes and objects work.

PROBLEM STATEMENT

In this lab, you will be building, with objects, a program that simulates a computer network. You will be the "system operator" of the network. You are going to build and maintain this network. To test the network that you have built, you will temporarily pretend to be a network user, and use the network without all the privileges that you have as the system operator.

Building a complete computer network from the ground up can be quite tedious. We will provide you with a set of functional object builders. You can build a simple network with these procedures and familiarize yourself with the basic network components.

The basic components of our network include **account**, **file server**, **host** and **file**. We will describe first the overall network structure, and then these basic components.

Network Structure

Figure 20-1 is a graphical representation of the simulated network in this lab. Each enclosed box represents an internal state. The major elements in the network are:

- a **file server** holds **accounts** and public programs (**executable files**)
- a **host** is attached to a **file server**, and contains an environment with a **wrapper** and an active **account** when someone is logged in.
- a **file** contains text or a procedure that the host or file-server can run. **file**.

The goodie file network.scm contains the class definitions for the basic network components, including cl-file-server, cl-host, cl-account, cl-file, cl-executable, cl-environment, cl-wrapper.

In this lab, you will create objects of these classes, connected as in the diagram, and then log in to your account on a host object. You will write some Scheme programs that will be stored in file objects in your account on the file server, and then run these programs. The following sections describe the interfaces to these objects and their interactions.

Account

A network **account** lets a user store and retrieve files, execute private programs, and utilize public services such as electronic mail. Every account has a name called the user ID. A user can gain access to his account by specifying the account's ID and the corresponding password. The internal data of an account include the **id** of the account, the **password**, the **user-name** and the **files**. Every account resides on a particular file server.

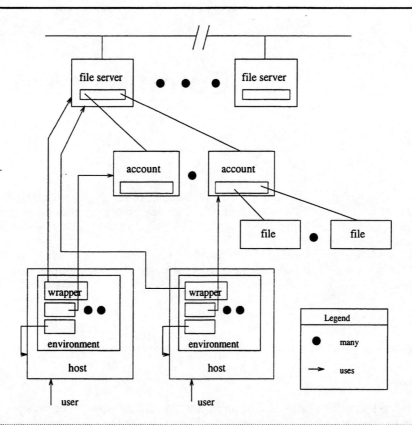

Figure 20-1   Network Structure

The following is a **class signature** for the c1-account class. In these network labs, we are naming all our classes c1-*xxx*. We do this because it can help you avoid confusion between classes and global variables.[1] Each of the methods of a class is presented in the same way procedures are. The name of the method is followed by its parameters, which are then described. Then the effect or returned value of the method is described.

CLASS c1-account

CONSTRUCTOR make *id password user-name*
ARGUMENTS
  • *id* is the account identifier
  • *password* is the account password
  • *user-name* is the name of the user
RETURNS   creates an account

METHOD user-name
RETURNS   the name of the user

METHOD add-file *file*
ARGUMENTS
  • *file* is a file
EFFECT   adds *file* the list of files for this account

---

[1] We didn't do this in the Adventure labs because there was little or no need for global variables.

METHOD remove-file *filename*

ARGUMENTS
- *filename* is a file name

EFFECT   removes the file with name *filename* from list of files

---

METHOD files

RETURNS   list of files in the account

METHOD get-file

ARGUMENTS
- *filename* is a file name

RETURNS   file with name *filename*

METHOD list-files

RETURNS   lists the names of the files

File Server

As the name implies, a **file server** is a computer that manages files for users. In a computer network, a group of file storage devices may contain many files of different users. The file server is responsible for storing files to and retrieving files from storage devices. This way, many users can share the same storage devices, making the network more cost efficient. The file server holds **accounts** and **public programs**, which are file objects. The class for file server objects is called cl-file-server. (It would be natural to call the class file-server, but it would be too easy to define a variable file-server and thus destroy the class definition.) The description of its methods and their arguments follows.

CLASS cl-file-server

CONSTRUCTOR make *name programs*

ARGUMENTS
- *name* is the name of the file server
- *programs* is the list of public program

EFFECT   creates a file server

METHOD init

EFFECT   adds itself to the file-server list

METHOD name

RETURNS   its name

METHOD add-account *account*

ARGUMENTS
- *account* is an account

EFFECT   adds *account* to the list of accounts

METHOD `remove-account` *accountname*

ARGUMENTS
- *accountname* is an account identifier

EFFECT   removes the account with name *accountname* from the list of accounts

---

METHOD `list-accounts`

RETURNS   lists the names of the accounts

METHOD `add-program` *prog*

ARGUMENTS
- *prog* is a program

EFFECT   adds *prog* to the list of programs

METHOD `remove-program` *progname*

ARGUMENTS
- *progname* is a program name

EFFECT   removes the program with name *progname* from the list of programs

---

METHOD `public-progs`

RETURNS   the list of public programs

METHOD `verify-password` *account password*

ARGUMENTS
- *account* is the name of a private or public program
- *password* is the password for *account*

EFFECT   if *password* is the password of *account*, returns the account, else #f

---

METHOD `sendmail` *email*

ARGUMENTS
- *email* is a mail object

EFFECT   runs `deliver-mail` with itself and the email as arguments (see the discussion of email in Lab 21)

Host

A **host** is a computer with which a single user can interact with her account. Users can only interact with their accounts through host machines. A host has a **file server**, **name**, and **account**.

CLASS `cl-host`

CONSTRUCTOR `make` *name file-server*

ARGUMENTS
- *name* is the name of the host
- *file-server* is the host to which it's attached

EFFECT   creates a host machine

METHOD name
RETURNS   its name

METHOD login *id password*
ARGUMENTS
- *id* is an account identifier
- *password* is the password for the account

EFFECT   if the password is correct, starts a wrapper and makes the account active

---

METHOD logout
EFFECT   removes the active account

METHOD run *progname arg1 ... argn*
ARGUMENTS
- *progname* is the name of a private or public program
- remaining arguments are passed to the program

EFFECT   runs the program with given arguments

METHOD wrapper *command arg1 ... argn*
ARGUMENTS
- *command* is the name of command
- remaining arguments are passed to the program

EFFECT   runs the wrapper command with given arguments

Once logged in, the user can run both his own programs and public programs, as follows:

```
(host 'run 'progname arg1 arg2 ... argn)
```

The host determines whether the program is private, and runs it. If not, it passes the file name to the wrapper (described below) to run it. To execute commands such as list-accounts, the user must type:

```
(host 'wrapper 'list-accounts)
```

This indicates that list-accounts is a command that the wrapper must handle.

Wrapper

A **wrapper** is an object that is like a layer wrapped around a file server. Each wrapper limits the user's access to the wrapped-in file server. This added security measure prevents users from destroying the content or the integrity of the file server. If a user wants to use some service on the file server, she sends messages to a wrapper that redirects them to the file server if they are public messages. Certain messages that the file servers recognize are rejected by the wrapper to prevent users from accessing them. A wrapper is created and inserted into a host when the user logs in. Each wrapper is wrapped around the file server to which the host is connected. As all wrappers are created inside host objects, they are only accessible through the environment object generated by the hosts.

CLASS cl-wrapper

CONSTRUCTOR make *file-server*
ARGUMENTS
- *file-server* is the host to which it's attached

EFFECT   creates a wrapper

METHOD run *env progname arg1 ... argn*
ARGUMENTS
- *env* is the environment of the account on the host
- *progname* is the name of a private or public program
- remaining arguments are passed to the program

EFFECT   runs the program with given arguments

METHOD list-accounts, verify-password, sendmail
ARGUMENTS
- remaining arguments are passed to the program

EFFECT   sends the message and arguments to the file server

METHOD add-account, remove-account, public-progs, accounts
EFFECT   informs the user the commands are privileged

Environment

An **environment** is an instance of class c1-environment. It keeps track of a list of variables and their corresponding values, much like an association list.

After a user logs into an account, the host automatically generates an environment with three variables: account, host, and wrapper, bound to three different objects, respectively the account of the active user, the local host machine, and the file server to which the host machine is connected. The environment is kept inside the host object and is destroyed when the user logs out.

CLASS c1-environment

CONSTRUCTOR make
EFFECT   creates an environment

METHOD add-variable *var value*
ARGUMENTS
- *var* is the name of a variable
- *value* is the value

EFFECT   adds *var* to list of variables

METHOD get-variable *var*
ARGUMENTS
- *var* is the name of a variable

RETURNS   the value of *var*

METHOD remove-variable *var*
ARGUMENTS
- *var* is a variable name

EFFECT   removes the variable with name *var* from list of variables

---

METHOD list
RETURNS   the list of names of the variables

File

A **file** is a collection of data stored as a unit. Files have different types; we will be concerned with executable and text files. For instance, the Scheme evaluator that you use to evaluate Scheme forms is an executable file whereas the goodie files for this lab are text files.

CLASS `cl-file`

CONSTRUCTOR make　*name content*
ARGUMENTS
- *name* is the name of the file
- *content* is its contents

EFFECT　　　creates a file

METHOD `type`
RETURNS　　　its type: `file`

METHOD `name`
RETURNS　　　its name

METHOD `executable?`
RETURNS　　　a Boolean indicating whether it is an executable file

---

METHOD `content`
RETURNS　　　the contents of the file

METHOD `set-content` *content*
ARGUMENTS
- *content* is the new file contents

EFFECT　　　change the file's contents

METHOD `copy` *name*
ARGUMENTS
- *name* is the name of the copy

RETURNS　　　a copy file of the contents with name *name*

There is a specialized form of file called an **executable file**, which responds #t to the `executable?` message. It is an instance of the class `cl-executable`. Its methods and constructor all have the same arguments as an instance of class `cl-file`.

Every executable has a procedure as its content. The first argument of this procedure one argument called the **environment**. We will use the convention that the contents of file foo will be a procedure named foo-body. An executable file object responds to the `executable?` message with #t and files that aren't executable with #f.

Building a network

We will build our network piece by piece. The initial stages of network construction must be performed by the system operator who has the ability to create special network components like the file server, accounts, and hosts. Only the system operator can send messages directly to the file server. The user must interact with the host, which in turn uses the file server.

Then, in order to run some programs, you must login as a user. (We'll assume a user named Joel is logged in during the examples.) To get information about the account—for example, id and user name—the user asks the host to return the account object which then itself will return the information. This is a common programming convention: if object a has an instance of b in one of its slots, the class provides a message b to access this instance. You can send a message foo to b by the following means: ((a 'b) 'foo). (a 'b) gets the b instance from a, which can then receive the foo message.[2]

We will write some executable files (instances of the class cl-executable) that examine text files. To be run, they must be added as files to the user's account. Then the user, when logged in, can run them on the host.

Here Joel runs the executable file exe-test that was just inserted into his account. The body of the file is simply a string that is returned as the value of the procedure.

```
> (host1 'run 'exe-test)
This is a test for the executable file
```

someinfo-body is the contents of a more interesting executable file in Joel's account, shown in Figure 20-2. In this example, someinfo-body, the content of the executable file someinfo, is defined before it is used in constructing an instance of class cl-executable.

```
> (define someinfo-body
    (lambda (env)
      (let ((account (env 'get-variable 'account)))
        (format #t "Your ID is ~s.~%" (account 'id)))))
> ((host1 'account) 'add-file
    (cl-executable 'make 'someinfo  someinfo-body))
> (host1 'run  'someinfo)
Your ID is joel.
```

Figure 20-2   Executables

As part of this lab you will write a more extensive version of someinfo that produces the following output:

```
You are Joel User and your user ID is joel.
    You are working on the host called host1,
    which is connected to the file server called fs1.
```

We'll call the file myinfo and the procedure myinfo-body:

PROCEDURE (myinfo-body *env*)

ARGUMENTS

- *env* is the standard environment of the account

EFFECT   prints the user name, account id, the current host, and the file server.

The host also passes commands to the wrapper, which are services that the file server handles. Look at the description of the wrapper to see how to list accounts on fs1.

We can also add a public program to a file server. It is common to have a public program that can find all files containing a particular string. The DOS and OS/2 find command does this; on Unix systems, the grep utility lets you find all files containing a string; moreover, it lets you specify general patterns of characters and "don't care" wild cards to permit a wide range of searching.

You will write find-body, a procedure that will be the content of an executable file, called find, that will be added to the public programs on the file server. find-body looks through all the files in the active account on the host. If a file is a text file (whose contents is a string), find-body then determines whether its argument, a string, is contained in the file. If so, it prints the file's contents.

---

[2] If you do this with all of the slots in an object, you will destroy the encapsulation—the hiding of data—that is one of the most important benefits of object-oriented programming. However, judicious use of this convention can improve a program by allowing you to make it more modular than it would otherwise be.

PROCEDURE (find-body *env str*)

ARGUMENTS
- *env* is the standard environment of the account
- *str* is a string

EFFECT   prints the contents of every file in the account in which the string *str* appears.

The contents of every text file is a string. The goodie `network.scm` provides `substring-of`:

PROCEDURE (substring-of *s1 s2*)

ARGUMENTS
- *s1* is a string
- *s2* is a string

RETURNS   a Boolean indicating whether the string *s1* appears in string *s2*

You can use `substring-of` to determine whether a string is anywhere in a file. For example, (substring-of "bc" "abcdef") ⇒ #t but (substring-of "cb" "abcdef") ⇒ #f. To run `find` as a public program, you must add it as a program to `fs1`.

BEFORE THE LAB

1. Find out how to set up the network by sending messages to network objects. Write down the forms that create a file-server, add accounts, create a host, login to the host, add files, and run the executable files.
2. Design `myinfo-body` and the forms that create `myinfo`. Write some tests for `myinfo`.
3. Design the executable file `find` and write test expressions for it.
4. Write down the forms that install `find` as a public program and run the program.
5. Find out how to logout from the host.

PITFALLS AND ADVICE

Executable files can only use the environment object and its content. The environment, however, contains variables holding the value of the account, the host, and the wrapper.

Network users are not allowed to send messages **directly** to any object except host objects and file objects. The content of all executable files written by network users can only use the provided environment object and its content. Users are allowed to instantiate file objects in the global environment.

CHECKPOINT

1. Does the file server run public programs?
2. Does the user directly send messages to the wrapper?
3. What are the local values (the slots) stored in an account object in the network?

DURING THE LAB

1. Before you can begin, you must first load the goodie file `network.scm`, which loads the routines used to generate the basic network components.
2. The first step is to create a file server called `fs1`, with no public programs. You must initialize it by sending it an `init` message.
   Then create accounts for Joel and Mary and add them to the file server.
   Create a host called `host1` connected to the file server.
   We need to login as Joel to his account on `host1`.

Create two text files (whose contents for simplicity will be a string), and add them to the account. Call the first one `test`: its content will be "Hello, world". Call the second `new`: its content will be "Farewell, cruel world".

3. Type in `myinfo-body`, create `myinfo`, the executable file, and try it out.

4. Create the executable file `find` and add it to the public programs on the file server. Get the host to run `find` with the string "ell" on the files in Joel's account.

AFTER THE LAB

1. At one point in this lab, Joel evaluated

   ```
   > (host1 'run 'exe-test)
   ```

   Give a list of the sequence of objects and messages involved in carrying out Joel's request.

DELIVERABLES

1. a printout showing that you have built the network, following the steps above
2. a listing of `myinfo` and output showing that it works
3. a listing of `find` and output showing that it works
4. your answer to the "After the Lab" question

FOR FURTHER INVESTIGATION

The network of file servers and hosts with files, accounts, and wrappers is a simplification of real systems. Write a brief comparison of the elements of the system we have built here to the elements on your favorite real operating system (such as Windows, OS/2, MacOS, Unix, or any other), and network (such as NetWare, NFS, Vines, Lantastic, or LAN Server). If you aren't familiar with any of these, you will need to do some research.

Deliverables: your report.

Computer Network Services

A computer network not only connects computers; it also provides **services** for its users. In this lab you will see how the object-oriented framework from Lab 20 can be extended to provide useful services.

WHAT YOU NEED TO KNOW

Read up through Section 6.2. Make sure you understand how classes and objects work. You must complete Lab 20 before starting this one.

PROBLEM STATEMENT

Lab 20 introduces the component classes of the network: **account, file server, host, environment, wrapper,** and **file**. There will be four tasks in this lab:

- changing user passwords: extending `cl-account` to allow users to change the account's password
- creating email: designing an executable file to access the electronic mail messages stored in a user's file
- transferring files between hosts (ftp): creating an object—an ftp connection—that can transfer files from one account to another
- creating a user executable file to do ftp: creating an executable file that creates the ftp connection between two accounts

There are references to the class definitions for the network objects throughout the lab. The definitions appear at the end of the lab.

The following is a list of the goodie files used by this lab:

- **network.scm** classes for basic network components, including `cl-file-server`, `cl-host`, `cl-account`, `cl-file`, `cl-executable`, `cl-environment`, `cl-wrapper`
- **netemail.scm** electronic mail, including `cl-email`, `cl-address`, `deliver-mail`, `file-email cl-address`, `deliver-mail`
- **netftp.scm** unfinished procedure `do-ftp`
- **nethelp.scm** alist procedures

Changing account passwords

For security reasons, network users are advised to change their password from time to time.[1] Presently, a password is assigned to an account when you create an instance of `cl-account` (shown in Program 21-2), but there is no way for a user to change the password afterwards. Noting the problem, you decide to add a new method to `cl-account` so that users can change their passwords. To ensure that the person who is changing the password is the owner of the account, the user must supply both the old and the new password to the password-changing method. For example, Joel is logged onto `host1` and he wants to change his password from `frobnitz` to `bafflegab`; he can change his password by typing in the Scheme form

```
> ((host1 'account) 'change-password 'frobnitz 'bafflegab)
```

---

[1] On many real networks, users are asked to change passwords about once a month.

The (host1 'account) returns the account object which then receives the change-password message. If the old password is **not** equal to the original password, the change-password method doesn't update the password to the new one, but displays a message to inform the user about the problem.

Many of the classes in this lab use the box-alist ADT shown in Figure 21-1.

Constructor

- (make-box-alist)
  Return a new alist in a box.

Accessors

- (box-alist-ref *balist*)
  Return contents of *balist*.

Mutators

- (add-box-alist! *balist key value*)
  Add key-value to the alist. If key already exists, update the value, otherwise, add a new pair.
- (remove-box-alist! *balist key*)
  Remove the pair for key *key* from the association list.

Figure 21-1   Abstract Data Type: box-alist

Electronic mail

Electronic mail is a popular communication medium in computer networks. Each "letter" in electronic mail is a message from one user to another. Users of a network can send messages from one account to another account much as mail can be sent from one location to another.

In our network, these messages are delivered to a file in the user's account, called the **mailbox**. This problem asks you to write an executable file (whose body is a Scheme procedure) that will examine the letters in the mail file. Electronic mail messages (email for short) are instances of the class cl-email.

CLASS cl-email

CONSTRUCTOR make *from-addr to-addr subject content*
ARGUMENTS
- *from-addr* is the address of the sender
- *to-addr* is the address of the receiver
- *subject* is the subject of the mail
- *content* is the content of the mail

EFFECT   creates an email object

METHOD from-addr
RETURNS   the address of the sender

METHOD to-addr
RETURNS   the address of the receiver

METHOD subject
RETURNS   the subject of the mail

METHOD content
RETURNS   the content of the mail

Addresses are also instances of the class `cl-address`.

CLASS `cl-address`

CONSTRUCTOR make *user-id file-server-name*
ARGUMENTS
- *user-id* is the id of the account
- *file-server-name* is the name of file server where the account is

EFFECT   creates an address

METHOD `user-id`
RETURNS   the user id

METHOD `file-server-name`
RETURNS   the file server name

To send mail, the user evaluates a form that makes a message object and then asks for that message to be sent.

```
> (host1 'wrapper 'sendmail
    (cl-email 'make
      (cl-address 'make 'acc1 'fs1)   ; from-address
      (cl-address 'make 'acc2 'fs2)   ; to-address
      'test-subject
      'test-content))
```

This causes the host to hand the `sendmail` message to the wrapper, which determines that `sendmail` is a public operation that the file server should handle. (The class definition of host appears in Programs 21-4 and 21-5.)

Email is distributed by file servers in our simulated network because users' accounts are installed in file servers. A file server (its class definition appears in Program 21-3) delivers a letter when given the message `sendmail` and a letter object. For example :

```
> (fs1 'sendmail
    (cl-email 'make
      (cl-address 'make 'acc1 'fs1)   ; from-address
      (cl-address 'make 'acc2 'fs2)   ; to-address
      'test-subject
      'test-content))
```

requests file server `fs1` to deliver a letter from account `acc1` on `fs1` to account `acc2` on `fs2`. The `sendmail` method is already written and is available to all users from all file servers through the wrappers.

The file server uses the procedure `deliver-mail` to handle the mail. When email arrives at an account, it is stored in a file named `mail`. The content of `mail` is always an association list with a number as the car and a letter object as the cdr of each pair. The procedure `file-email` inserts email into an account.

To implement email, you will design an executable file object called `mail-exe` so that a user can run it from the host as follows:
- display the letters in the mailbox

  `(host1 'run 'mail-exe 'list-letters)`

- display the from-address, to-address, subject, and content of letter number 1

  `(host1 'run 'mail-exe 'read-letter 1)`

- remove letter 1 from the mailbox

  `(host1 'run 'mail-exe 'remove-letter 1)`

You will write a procedure that will be the body of mail-exe. You can call it mail-exe-body; it should act as follows:

PROCEDURE (mail-exe-body *env message . args*)

ARGUMENTS
- *env* is the standard environment of the account
- *message* is one of list-letters, read-letter, or remove-letter
- *args* is the list of the remaining arguments

EFFECT   performs the designated mail command

The message list-letters should display No letters if the file called mail does not exist or if mail does not contain any letter. Otherwise, the list of letters should be displayed in the following format :

> *letter number   from-address's user id   subject*
> *letter number   from-address's user id   subject*
> .
> .

For example :

5	acc1	Scheme question
3	clee	Re: comment on Network Lab
2	a2d192	sleeping in Undergrad lab

read-email and remove-email should do nothing if the given letter number does not exist. mail-exe should display the address, subject and content during read-email in anyway you like, as long as you can tell the different items apart. You don't have to understand deliver-mail for this problem. Reading file-email will explain the structure of the mail file.

File transfer

The letter can be transported from one server to another because of a global association list called file-servers defined in the goodie file network.scm. The sender file server looks up the receiver file server from file-servers and sends the letter to the receiver file server. The receiver file server then tries to deliver the letter to the correct account. Read and understand the email delivering procedures: deliver-mail is shown in Program 21-6 and file-email is shown in Program 21-7; both are in netemail.scm. You are going to write a similar service for the file servers to send files over the network.

A special kind of network called the *Internet* has a popular service called **ftp**. ftp uses a technique called the File Transfer Protocol (FTP) to transfer files across the network. In this problem, you are going to implement and install a simulated version of this service in the network.

You are given an unfinished procedure do-ftp in the file netftp.scm, shown in Program 21-1. You are going write the class definition for cl-ftp according to the following specifications.

ftp, just like email, is a service that can be used between two accounts located in two different file servers. However, unlike email, a user needs to know the remote account's password before he or she can transfer files from the local account to the remote account or vice versa. As files are treated as private properties owned by the account's user, one must have the necessary permission before accessing other's private property. With ftp, a user can copy files to and from a different account. In reality, ftp is a service that a user begins by connecting to another file-server, and then reads and writes files from the other server.

```
(define do-ftp
  (lambda (account password)
    (if (account 'verify-password password)
      (cl-ftp 'make account)
      (error (list (file-server 'name) 'ftp)
             "ftp failed.  incorrect password"))))
```

Program 21-1   The ftp program

In our simulation, do-ftp returns an object, an ftp connection, which is an instance of class cl-ftp, to which you can send messages to perform file transfer.

account is the remote account, the account the user is trying to access with ftp. (The local account, on the other hand, is the account from which the user is requesting the ftp service). password is the password for the remote account. The first step for do-ftp is to verify the password for the account. Then it creates the connection, which is an object of class cl-ftp.

To begin an ftp session, create the ftp connection:

```
(let ((connection (do-ftp acc2 'acc2-password)))
  ....
  )
```

do-ftp should create an object that will respond to the messages: ftp-read, ftp-write, ftp-list. You should write a class cl-ftp, and do-ftp can instantiate it, resulting in an ftp connection object. While the connection exists, you can perform file transfer by sending messages to it, as described in its class signature.

CLASS cl-ftp

CONSTRUCTOR make *account*

ARGUMENTS
  • *account* is the remote account

EFFECT   creates an ftp connection

METHOD ftp-read *filename-list*

ARGUMENTS
  • *filename-list* is a list of the names of files in the remote account

RETURNS   retrieves from the remote account the file objects named in *filename-list* and returns them in a list.

METHOD ftp-write *files*

ARGUMENTS
  • *file* is a list of file objects

RETURNS   the file objects in the list *files* into the remote account and returns the empty list.

METHOD ftp-list

RETURNS   returns the list of filenames in the remote account

---

You will have to modify the cl-wrapper class (shown in Program 21-8) to allow the user to execute the ftp command. Like all such commands, it will be passed to the file server, which will evaluate do-ftp with the appropriate arguments.

```
(define connection (host1 'wrapper 'ftp account password))
```

returns the connection to which you can send messages to perform file transfer.

You will have to modify the cl-file-server class to call do-ftp. send messages to perform file transfer.

Building a more useful ftp program

In this problem you will create an executable file object called ftp-exec so that the user can do the following:

```
> (host1 'run 'ftp-exec
    acc2 'acc2-password 'read (list 'file-a 'file-c))
```

to read files file-a and file-c from an account called acc2 located in file server fs2 and write them into the local account.

```
> (host1 'run 'ftp-exec
    acc2 'acc2-password 'write (list file1 file2))
```

writes local files called `file1` and `file2` to the remote account called `acc2` located in file server `fs2`. (The local files are file objects contained in the local account.)

```
> (host1 'run 'ftp-exec
    acc2 'acc2-password 'list)
```

lists the files contained in the remote account.

`ftp-exec-body`, the procedure that is the content of `ftp-exec`, should have the following description:

PROCEDURE (`ftp-exec-body` *env to-account password command . args*)

ARGUMENTS
- *env* is the standard environment of the account
- *to-account* is the destination account
- *password* is the password of the destination account
- *command* is one of `read`, `write`, or `list`
- *args* is the list of the remaining arguments

EFFECT   performs the designated ftp command

Like `do-ftp`, `ftp-exec` should check that the password for the source account is valid. The `ftp-exec` executable should simply return an error for any command that doesn't make sense. Also it should return an error for any reference to non-existent files.

BEFORE THE LAB

Before you start to write any code, please read the section **Pitfalls** which describes some of the common mistakes and some techniques that makes testing your code easier.

1. Design the modifications to `cl-account` to allow password changing.
2. Design `mail-exe`, the executable file that handles email.
3. Design `do-ftp` and `cl-ftp`, plus the modifications to `cl-file-server` and `cl-wrapper`.
4. Design `ftp-exec`.

For all the above, write out test forms that demonstrate the operations intended.

PITFALLS AND ADVICE

1. **Structure of general network objects** A special technique is used in network object classes to allow every object to refer to itself. This is particularly useful when objects need to pass themselves to another object as arguments. The `self` variable is bound to the object itself in any instance of a class. The methods in our class definitions have parameters in the form (`message . args`)—this means that at least one argument will be specified, and possibly more. `message` is bound to the first argument, and `args` is bound to the list of the remaining arguments.
   For an example of how an object can pass itself to another object, refer to the `login` method in the class `cl-host`. In that code the object, `self`, is added to the environment as the value of `host`.

2. **When updating classes** *After updating classes, reload the entire system, else your objects may behave incorrectly. Changing the class definition does not change existing objects.* Even objects that are not instances of the classes you have just changed may work improperly if not re-created. For instance, after updating the `cl-file-server` class, you should not only re-instantiate *all* your file servers, but also re-instantiate the host machines. The reason is that the host objects have internal states that refers to a file server. If you simply re-instantiate the file servers and not the host objects, your host objects will be referring to the file servers objects that are built before you changed `cl-file-server`.

3. **Put frequently used Scheme forms in file(s)** Put all the object building Scheme forms in file(s) so that you do not have to retype the definitions every time you change classes. The next time after you have changed a class, simply re-evaluate the file(s) to re-instantiate the objects.

Use a file (or many files if necessary) to contain test procedures and test statements. You can save a lot of time by re-evaluating files instead of manually typing the test statements over and over again. For an example of the use of test files, refer to the goodie file `nettest.scm`.

4. **Keep procedures short** Lengthy Scheme forms are hard to debug, especially if they are nested in an object. To keep classes short and easy to read, try to isolate the methods that are more than 20 lines in length. For examples, refer to the `sendmail` method in `cl-file-server` and the routines in the helper goodie file `netemail.scm`.

CHECKPOINT

1. When you evaluate `(foo 1)`, given that `foo` is defined as:

   `(define foo (lambda (x . args) ...))`

   What is the value of `args`?
2. In the `case` form, the first element in a clause is list of keys. Why is it a list of keys and not just a single key?
3. An object created from a class specified by `define-class` calls `error` when it does not have the method requested. Give a reason why you might want to specify your own `else` method.

DURING THE LAB

1. **Changing passwords**

   a. Use a separate file to contain the modified version of `cl-account` and include test statements to prove that the new `cl-account` works according to the above specification. Include `format` statements in your test code so that the marker can interpret the result easily. Example test statements appear in Figure 21-2.

   b. Print out a copy of your modified `cl-account` class along with the test statements and a copy of the test log. Make sure you know how to create an account object and how to add files to and remove files from an account. Make sure you know how to make file objects, and how to retrieve and change their contents. You should experiment with `cl-account` and `cl-file` as the system operator, (As the system operator, you are allowed to directly send messages to objects).

2. **Email**

   a. Create a file server object and connect a host object to it. Create two account objects for two users and add them to the file server. As a user, send a letter from one account to the other account. Show that the other user has received the letter by displaying its addresses, subject and content. Get a printout of the statements you have used to accomplish the requested result. Do not print the result log.

   b. Create two file server objects, two host objects, and two account objects. Connect one host to each file server and insert one account into each file server. Get one user from one file server to send a letter to the other user in the other file server.

   c. After you have got `mail-exe` working, insert it into one or two file servers so that `mail-exe` becomes public. The users with accounts in the file servers installed with `mail-exe` should then be able to use the following command to manipulate their email :

      `(host1 'wrapper 'mail-exe 'list-letters)`

   Use a separate file for creating the `mail-exe` executable file and include your test statements in the same file. Use the same format for the test statements as in the password problem. Get a printout of the code you wrote, your test file, and the test log.

3. **ftp**

   a. After you have finished `do-ftp`, create 2 file server objects, 2 host objects and 2 account objects. Connect a host to each file server and insert an account in each file server. Create a few files and install them in the accounts. As the system operator, test out `do-ftp` to see if it works properly.

b. If all is working fine, add a new method called `ftp` to `cl-file-server` that gathers the appropriate arguments and uses `do-ftp` to carry out the ftp operation. Your new method should look something like this :

```
(ftp
    .
    .

    ((do-ftp me ???) ..)))
```

Get a printout of the `do-ftp` code, the modified file-server, and test output showing that both work.

4. **Building a more useful ftp program**

Type in your `ftp-exec` procedure and test it out, demonstrating that it responds as described above.

```
(format #t
    "Change-password method for cl-account~%")
(format #t
  "creating : file server fs1, host host1 and account acc1~%")
(define fs1 (cl-file-server 'fs1 '()))
    .
    .

(format #t "logging into acc1 with original-password~%")
(host1 'login 'acc1 'original-password)
    .
    .

(format #t
  "changing password from original-password to new-password~%")
((host1 'account) 'change-password
  'original-password 'new-password)
    .
    .

(format #t "logging into acc1 with new-password~%"))
(host1 'login 'acc1 'new-password)
```

Figure 21-2   Test statements

AFTER THE LAB

Perhaps the two operations `run` and `wrapper` in the `cl-host` could be combined. Describe why or why not. Indicate the possible technical problems and some of the benefits and problems of combining the two.

DELIVERABLES

1. Passwords: a copy of your modified `cl-account` class along with the test statements and a copy of the test log
2. Email: printout of the code you wrote, your test file and the test log
3. File transfer: printout of the `do-ftp` code, the modified class `cl-file-server`, and the modified class `cl-wrapper`, and test output showing that they work
4. ftp program: printout of the finished `ftp-exec` procedure and test output showing that it works

FOR FURTHER INVESTIGATION

Working as the system operator is really not that exciting. So, let's pretend that you are a crazed programmer who is going to write a virus! Computer viruses are programs that can duplicate themselves (multiply) and sometimes cause serious damage to their environment, such as erasing all the files in the local file storage area. Viruses have caused enormous damage to many users across the world. We do not condone such anti-social activities that bring disrepute to all computer programmers and interfere with the legitimate work of users. We are going to use this example because it will give you some understanding of how programs as data in files can be altered by other programs. It will also give you an idea of the damage that viruses can do.

The virus that you are going to write is going to be self-replicating. In other words, it can spread its virus-like behavior to uninfected files. In our case, the virus must an executable file and can only infect another executable files.

First, we shall start up with a "mild" virus that simply spreads and does no harm.

You are going to write a procedure called `infect` that has the following syntax :

PROCEDURE (`infect` *executable*)

ARGUMENTS

  • *executable* is an executable file

RETURNS   an infected executable file

It takes an executable file and returns another executable that has a content that apparently behaves just like the original executable's content. The only exception is that the "infected" executable's content(a procedure), after getting the environment object as its argument, infects all the other executable file objects in the local account. Only after infecting all the other executables does the infected executable executes its "normal" operation. For example, the infected version of `myinfo` used in Lab 20 should:

  • infect all uninfected executables, then
  • carry out the normal "myinfo" operation of displaying the active account's information

when it is executed. The two operations described above are necessary for the virus to multiply and to remain undetected.

The content of the infected object should look something like this (yours may look a little different) :

```
((content)
 (lambda (env)
   ; procedures that
   ; infect other executables
   ; YOU ARE GOING TO WRITE THIS
   ((original-executable 'content) env)
))
```

Also, to prevent a virus from infecting an already infected executable, all infected executable objects return `infected-executable` when given the `type` message. So, assuming we have an executable called `myinfo` declared in the global environment, we should get the following results :

```
> (define infected-myinfo (infect myinfo))
> (infected-myinfo 'type)
infected-executable
```

Implement `infect` so that the infected executable accepts two methods: `type` and `content`, and passes the rest to the original executable file. The `'content` method should return the content of the virus object. DO NOT attempt to mutate the content of the original executable file.

Create an account and some executable files. Infect one of of the executable files and execute it. If you have implemented `infect` correctly, you should be able to infect the other files.

To make the virus nastier, you can modify `infect` so that the infected executable erases all files in the local account after the fifth time the infected executable receives the `content` message. This way, you can leave time for the infected executables to infect other executables, and maybe some of them will be ftp'ed to another account! Each infected executable should remain harmless until the fifth execution is carried out.

As the system operator, you dedicate yourself in combating the virus that you found on the network. Write a virus scan program called `virus-scan` that will return a list of all the infected executable files in the local account. This should be straightforward.

The way we have implemented `infect` should allow one to retrieve the original, uninfected content from an infected executable. Write a virus cleaning program called `virus-clean` that will return all the infected executables in the local account back to normal.

To make the virus so that it can last longer, modify `infect` so that it only erases all the files after the fifth execution 30% of the time. Call this newly modified procedure `cl-longlasting-virus`. To test the infected executables produced by `cl-longlasting-virus`, use the `random-seed` command to choose a set of "random" numbers. Reset the random seed before you execute the infected executable and you should be able to predict the number of execution needed before all the files in the account are removed.

There is a way to make the virus both undetectable by the current version of `virus-scan` and uncleanable by the current version of `virus-clean`. Modify `infect` to create a procedure called `cl-deadly-virus` that cannot be scanned or cleaned.

Put your `infect`, `virus-scan`, `virus-clean`, `cl-longlasting-virus` and `cl-deadly-virus` procedures in a separate file along with the test statements that will prove your procedures to be working properly.

Is it possible to scan and clean the deadly virus (provided that cleaning a virus includes removing the infected file if the virus is inseparable from the original executable)? If so, write a paragraph describing how they can be done. (**Hint** : use ftp.)

Deliverables: a printout of your test file, the test log and your answer to the above questions

```
(define-class cl-account
  (constructor-arguments id password user-name)
  (slots (files (make-box-alist)))
  (methods (message . args)
   ((user-name) user-name)
   ((id) id)
   ((files) (box-alist-ref files))
   ((verify-password) (eqv? password (car args)))
   ((add-file)
    (let ((new-file (car args)))
      (add-box-alist! files (new-file 'name) new-file)))
   ((remove-file)
    (let ((file-name (car args)))
      (remove-box-alist! files file-name)))
   ((get-file)
    (let ((file-name (car args))
          (lfiles (box-alist-ref files)))
      (let ((result (assv file-name lfiles)))
        (if result (cdr result) #f))))
   ((list-files) (map (lambda (apair) (car apair))
                   (box-alist-ref files)))))
```

Program 21-2   The class definition for account

```
;global declaration of an association list of file servers
(define file-servers (make-box-alist))

(define-class cl-file-server
  (slots (accounts (make-box-alist))
         (public-progs (make-box-alist)) (self #f))
  (constructor-arguments name programs)
  (methods (message . args)
   ((init)
    (set! self (car args))
    (set! public-progs
      (map (lambda (prog) (cons (prog 'name) prog))
        programs))
    (add-alist! file-servers name self))
   (name name)
   (list-accounts
    (map (lambda (x) ((cdr x) 'id)) (box-alist-ref accounts)))
   ((accounts) (box-alist-ref accounts))
   ((public-progs) (box-alist-ref public-progs))
   ((add-account)
    (add-box-alist! accounts ((car args) 'id) (car args)))
   ((remove-account)
    (remove-box-alist! accounts (car args)))
   ((verify-password)
     (let ((result (assv (car args) (box-alist-ref accounts))))
       (if result
         (if ((cdr result) 'verify-password (car (cdr args)))
           (cdr result)
           #f)
         #f)))
   ((add-program)
     (let ((program (car args)))
       (add-box-alist! public-progs
           (program 'name) program)))
   ((remove-program)
    (let ((program-name (car args)))
      (remove-box-alist! public-progs program-name)))
   ((sendmail) (deliver-mail self (car args)))))
```

Program 21-3   The class definition for file server

```
(define-class cl-host
  (constructor-arguments name file-server)
  (slots (account #f) (env #f) (self #f))
  (methods (message . args)
   ((init) (set! self (car args)))
   ((name) name)
   ((login)
    (let ((user-id (car args))
          (password (car (cdr args))))
      (if (not account)
          (let ((result (file-server 'verify-password
                                     user-id password)))
            (if result
                (begin
                  (set! account result)
                  (set! env (cl-environment 'make))
                  (env 'add-variable 'account account)
                  (env 'add-variable 'host self)
                  (env 'add-variable 'wrapper
                    (cl-wrapper 'make file-server))
                  (format #t "Welcome to ~a~%" (file-server 'name)))
                (begin
                  (format #t "Can't let you login.")
                  (format #t "You must have typed something wrong~%")))
          (format #t "You can't login twice~%")))))
   ((logout)
    (if account
        (begin
          (format #t "Later ~a!   Logged out~%" (account 'user-name))
          (set! account #f)
          (set! env #f))
        (error (list name message) "No user at the moment")))
   ((account)
    (if (not account)
        (error (list name message) "No user at the moment")
        account))
```

```
((run)
 (if (not account)
     (error (list name message) "No user at the moment")
     (let ((name (car args))
           (files (account 'files)))
       (let ((result (assv name files)))
         (if result
             (let ((prog (cdr result)))
               (if (prog 'executable?)
                   (apply (prog 'content)
                          (cons env (cdr args)))
                   #f))
             (let ((wrapper (env 'get-variable 'wrapper)))
               (apply wrapper (cons 'run (cons env args)))))))))
((wrapper)
 (if (not account)
     (error (list name message) "No user at the moment")
     (let ((name (car args))
           (wrapper (env 'get-variable 'wrapper)))
       (apply wrapper args))))))
```

Program 21-5   The class definition for host, part 2

```
;- delivers a message to its destination.
(define deliver-mail
  (lambda (file-server email)
    (let*
      ((to-addr     (email 'to-addr))
       (to-server-n (to-addr 'file-server-name))
       (to-server   (assv to-server-n (box-alist-ref file-servers)))
       (to-user     (to-addr 'user-id))
       (from-addr   (email 'from-addr))
       (from-server-n (from-addr 'file-server-name))
       (from-server
         (assv from-server-n (box-alist-ref file-servers)))
       (from-user   (from-addr 'user-id)))
      (if (legal-addresses from-server from-user to-server to-user)
          (if (eqv? to-server-n (file-server 'name)) ; local
              (file-email
                (cdr (assv to-user (file-server 'accounts))) email)
              ((cdr (assv from-server (box-alist-ref file-servers)))
               'sendmail email))
          (format #t "Bad addresses: ~a ~a ~a ~a ~%"
            from-server-n from-user to-server-n to-user)))))
(define legal-addresses
  (lambda (from-server from-user to-server to-user)
    (and from-server to-server
         (assv from-user ((cdr from-server) 'accounts))
         (assv to-user ((cdr to-server) 'accounts)))))
```

Program 21-6   Delivering mail

```
(define file-email
  (lambda (account email)
    (let ((mail (account 'get-file 'mail)))
      (if (or (not mail) (null? (mail 'content)))
        ;;; mail file not found or empty
        (begin
          (set! mail (cl-file 'make 'mail (list (cons 1 email))))
          (account 'add-file mail))
        (let* ((mail-content (mail 'content))
               (newmail-num  (+ (car (car mail-content)) 1)))
          (set! mail-content
            (cons (cons newmail-num email) mail-content))
          (mail 'set-content mail-content))))))
```

Program 21-7   Filing mail

```
;;; the wrapper allows a user to execute public programs and
;;; prohibits users from using privileged file-server messages
(define-class cl-wrapper
  (constructor-arguments file-server)
  (methods (message . args)
   ((run) ;;; run public program
    (let ((public-progs (file-server 'public-progs)))
      (let ((result (assv (car (cdr args)) public-progs)))
        (if result
          (apply ((cdr result) 'content)
            (cons (car args) (cdr (cdr args))))
          (error (list 'a-wrapper 'run message)
            (format #f "No such program ã" (car args)))))))
   ;; public message
   ((name list-accounts verify-password sendmail)
    (apply file-server (cons message args)))
   ;; privileged message
   ((add-account remove-account public-progs accounts)
    (error (list 'a-wrapper message)
           "You don't have enough privilege to do that"))))
```

Program 21-8   The class definition for wrapper

```
(define-class cl-file
  (constructor-arguments name content)
  (methods (message . args)
   ((type) 'file)
   ((name) name)
   ((executable)? #f)
   ((content) content)
   ((set-content) (set! content (car args)))
   ((copy) (cl-file 'make (car args) content))))
```

Program 21-9   The class definition for file

```
(define-class cl-executable
  (constructor-arguments name content)
  (slots (myfile (cl-file 'make name content)))
  (methods (message . args)
   ((executable?) #t)
   (else (myfile message)))))
```

Program 21-10   The class definition for executable

```
(define-class cl-environment
  (slots (variables (make-box-alist)))
  (methods (message . args)
   ((add-variable)
    (add-box-alist! variables (car args) (car (cdr args))))
   ((get-variable)
    (let ((variables (box-alist-ref variables)))
      (let ((result (assv (car args) variables)))
        (if result (cdr result) #f))))
   ((list)
    (map (lambda (apair) (car apair)) variables))
   ((remove-variable)
    (remove-box-alist! variables (car args))))))
```

Program 21-11   The class definition for environment

```
(define make-box-alist
  (lambda ()
    (make-box '())))

; add-box-alist! - adds an item to the alist with mutation
; if the item already exists, update value, otherwise, adds item
;                       to the front of the list

(define add-box-alist!
  (lambda (balist key value)
    (if (not (box? balist))
        (error 'add-alist! "alist is not boxed")
        (let* ((alist (box-ref balist)))
               (result (assv key alist)))
          (if result
            (set-cdr! result value)
            (box-set! balist
              (cons (cons key value) alist)))))))

; remove-box-alist - removes an item from the association list

(define remove-box-alist!
 (lambda (balist key)
    (if (not (box? balist))
        (error 'remove-box-alist! "alist is not boxed")
        (box-set! balist
          (remove-alist-help (box-ref balist) key)))))

(define remove-alist-help
  (lambda (alist key)
    (if (null? alist)
        (error 'remove-box-alist! "key ā not found" key)
        (if (eqv? (car (car alist)) key)
          (cdr alist)
          (cons (car alist) (remove-alist (cdr alist) key))))))

(define box-alist-ref
  (lambda (balist)
    (box-ref balist)))
```

Program 21-12   Implementation of the box-alist ADT

```
(define-class cl-email
  (constructor-arguments from-addr to-addr subject content)
  (methods (message)
   ((from-addr) from-addr)
   ((to-addr) to-addr)
   ((subject) subject)
   ((content) content)))
```

Program 21-13   The class definition for email

```
(define-class cl-address
  (constructor-arguments user-id file-server-name)
  (methods (message)
   ((user-id) user-id)
   ((file-server-name) file-server-name)))
```

Program 21-14   The class definition for address

Lab 22

Object-Oriented Drawing

Many people have used a drawing program such as MacDraw. Such programs let you select shapes, place them into the diagram you are building, and transform them (by scaling and translation) as you wish. In this lab, we are going to build a simple drawing package, using object-oriented ideas. By doing so, we will study the way Scheme implements objects.

WHAT YOU NEED TO KNOW

Read up to Section 6.3, paying particular attention to the discussion of delegation on page 333. Review your graphic transformation labs.

PROBLEM STATEMENT

In 1963, a computer scientist named Ivan Sutherland wrote a Ph.D. thesis in which he described a program named Sketchpad that allowed the user to draw shapes on the screen. Sketchpad was one of the earliest programs to use object-oriented concepts: the user created instances of various master shapes, and transformed them as needed. Although Sketchpad was a curiosity, it was the inspiration for drawing programs such as MacDraw, and CAD (computer-assisted design) programs such as AutoCAD.

Drawing programs are said to be object-oriented, in contrast to painting programs such as MacPaint and PC Paintbrush, in which the fundamental operation is to turn **pixels**—individual spots on the screen or paper—on or off. The object orientation comes from the fact that the program works with the *objects* themselves, rather than with the pixels.

We have learned a slightly different meaning of "object-oriented." To us, an object-oriented program is one that operates by sending *messages* to objects; recall the banking example from Chapter 6.

How is this meaning of object orientation relevant to the drawing problem? A drawing program places various shapes on the screen. Each shape has a lower left corner (the **reference point**); any shape can be translated or scaled. But different shapes are drawn differently: a triangle will have three vertices, whereas a square has four; a circle might be characterized by a centre point and a radius.

Thus, for example, if we wish to draw a rectangle, we might write the following code:

```
(set! rect1 (rectangle 'make))
(rect1 'scale 100)
(rect1 'translate-x 50)
(rect1 'translate-y 75)
(rect1 'aspect-ratio 0.5))
(rect1 'draw)
```

In this example, we have asked for a rectangle that is scaled by a factor of 100, and translated to (50, 75). The rectangle has an **aspect ratio** of 0.5, which means that it will be half as wide as it is high: thus the final rectangle will be 50 units wide and 100 units high. We have then commanded the rectangle to draw itself.

We can describe our various shapes with objects, as we did with turtles. However, we want to leave the program fairly open-ended, so that we can easily add new shapes as the need arises. Further, sometimes two shapes are similar. For example, a filled square is just like an unfilled one, except that the interior, rather than being white, is darkened. But it would still look as though we have to write methods for each message.

In object-oriented programming, the concept of **delegation** lets us organize things so as to avoid much of the rewriting. The idea is fairly simple: we will have not only rectangle objects, but also shape objects; if we design things so that any messages that are not understood by rectangle objects are passed on to the shape object, then we can implement rectangle objects by only supplying needed methods. What are they? Two rectangle methods are needed, for the aspect-ratio and draw messages. The other messages, such as scaling and translation, can be passed on to the shape object for handling there.

For this to work properly, the shape object has to be able to tell us its current scaling and translation parameters. Therefore, we will have a message, `transforms`, that can be sent to a shape, and which will return a list containing the translation and scaling information. For example, in the above rectangle situation, the result of the `transforms` message would be (100 100 50 75). (We have separate scaling information for *x* and *y*, for reasons explained below.)

We can put all of this together in the class definition for shapes shown in Program 22-1. We have added a method `set-transforms`, which can be used to do everything at once.

```
(define-class shape
  (slots (x 0) (y 0) (scale-x 1) (scale-y 1))
  (methods (message . args)
   ((scale)
    (set! scale-x (car args))
    (set! scale-y (list-ref args 1)))
   ((translate-x)
    (set! x (car args)))
   ((translate-y)
    (set! y (car args)))
   ((transforms)
    (list scale-x scale-y x y))
   ((set-transforms)
    (set! scale-x (car args))
    (set! scale-y (list-ref args 1))
    (set! x (list-ref args 2))
    (set! y (list-ref args 3)))))
```

Program 22-1   A shape class

A rectangle has within it a shape, a value returned by calling (shape 'make), to handle all of the work of managing transforms. What rectangles know in addition to their shape are (a) the aspect ratio, and (b) how to draw a rectangle of a given aspect ratio.

```
(define-class rectangle
  (slots (aspect 1) (myshape (shape 'make)))
  (methods (message . args)
  ((aspect-ratio)
   (set! aspect (car args)))
  ((get-aspect)
   aspect)
  ((draw)
   (let ((xforms (myshape 'transforms)))
     ... do the drawing, using xforms ...))
  ((set-transforms)
   ... make sure that first two elements are the same
   ... scalex=scaley
   ... if not, error
   ... if ok, pass on to myshape.....
  (else
   (apply myshape message args)....)
```

Program 22-2   A rectangle class

BEFORE THE LAB

1. Finish off the `rectangle` class (i.e., write the code that does the drawing). `set-transforms` should not implicitly change the aspect-ratio!
2. Define a `square` object that contains a rectangle object (just as rectangles contain shapes). Your square object should provide its own `aspect-ratio` method (setting the aspect ratio for a square should result in an error, of course), but should pass off all other messages to its rectangle.
3. Define a `triangle` object. Assume that the triangle is a right triangle for simplicity and that the two edges joined by a right angle are aligned with the coordinate axes.

CHECKPOINT

1. How would you build a shape that had several parts?
2. What is one major difference between a procedure with state and one without state?
3. What would `args` be bound to if we evaluate (`rect1` '`set-transforms 1`)?

DURING THE LAB

1. Type in the `shape` and `rectangle` classes, and make sure that they work. Produce printouts that demonstrate this.
2. Type in the `square` class, and make sure that it works. You may not make any modifications whatsoever to the classes you wrote in the previous step. Again, produce printouts.
3. Now do the same for your `triangle` class, producing printouts.
4. So far, the scaling we have done is of the variety known as *isotropic*, in which x and y are scaled by the same amount. We can also do *anisotropic* scaling, in which different scale factors are used. Modify your shape class to support anisotropic scaling. (Add `scale-x` and `scale-y` methods. Leave the `scale` method there, in order to support isotropic scaling.) You may not make any modifications to any of the other object classes (`rectangle`, `square`, or `triangle`). Produce printouts that demonstrate that your modifications work.
5. Define a filled rectangle object type that contains a rectangle. This class may only have a `draw` method. A filled rectangle is "filled" with some pattern to make it black. There are many ways to do this; you need not make it completely black, just black enough to be distinguished easily from an unfilled rectangle. The "filler" needs to know the aspect-ratio of the rectangle, so the rectangle object returns that value in response to a `get-aspect` message.

AFTER THE LAB

1. We defined our program as a group of objects, each of which "knows" how to do one sort of drawing. (shapes can't really draw, but the principle is the same.) Each object contains only that code that *has* to be written.
   What makes this work in Scheme is environments. Draw a snapshot that shows what happens when you Scheme evaluates the sequence

   ```
   (define r (rectangle 'make))
   (r 'aspect-ratio 2)
   ```

2. Suppose you send a `scale` message to a filled rectangle object. Write a brief explanation of the process that goes on in handling this message.
3. Suppose you were implementing a `filled-square` object type. Would it make more sense to make this a kind of filled rectangle, or a kind of square? Write a brief explanation of how you would go about defining filled squares, with a justification of your choice. (Note: this is a difficult question to answer correctly!)

DELIVERABLES

1. listings of the `rectangle`, `triangle`, `square`, `filled-rectangle`, and their modified `shape` classes
2. all drawings they were asked to print in the during the lab part
3. answers to the "After the Lab" part

FOR FURTHER INVESTIGATION

1. Write a "top-level" program for your drawing package. Your top-level will read in command lines such as

```
(rectangle)
(scale 100)
(translate 50 75)
(draw)
quit
```

and will carry out the commands.

Your top-level will keep track of a "current object." In the above example, the first command creates a rectangle and makes it current. You must remember whether or not an object is current: scaling and translation only make sense when you're dealing with an object, but starting a new object doesn't make sense if you haven't drawn the previous one.[1]

This problem bears some thinking about: we're designing a simple picture language whose commands look like Scheme, but they're not Scheme. Your top-level program, not Scheme, reads each command and decides what to do with it.

2. Add an `undo` command to your top-level. The easiest way to do this is to keep a list of the objects, with the most recently drawn one at the front. `undo` can then be implemented by deleting the front element of the list, and redrawing all the objects left on the list.

Deliverables: The listing of your "top-level" program and a transcript demonstrating it working. For the `undo` command, provide a listing of the program and a transcript. In both cases, provide plots showing the effects of some commands.

---

[1] In this sense, your program is **modal**: either there is a current object, in which case you can transform or draw it, or there is not, in which case you can create a new object. Modality is generally considered a poor design appproach for modern user interfaces, because it forces the user to remember the current state of the system. A typical drawing program allows the user to select an object and then apply transformations to it, or to create a new object, at any time.

Lab 23
Exploring EBNF

OBJECTIVES

Extended Backus-Naur Form (EBNF) is a tool for defining the inputs to a program. An EBNF specification tells you what inputs the program is prepared to process (provided, of course, that the program matches the specification).

This lab gives you practice with EBNF. It provides you with software that reads EBNF rules and then generates random sentences that the EBNF specifies. This lets you debug your rules, and gives you an understanding of what you are specifying.

WHAT YOU NEED TO KNOW

Read up through Section 7.1. Make sure you understand what EBNF is used for, and how it works.

PROBLEM STATEMENT

A typical EBNF rule looks something like this:

```
category:        thing1 | ( [thing2] {thing3} ) | "whatever"
```

This defines a category of things called category in terms of other categories: thing1, thing2, and thing3.

- | means "or".
- [...] means "optionally".
- {...} means "0 or more repetitions".
- "..." is used to show text that is written as-is in the program.
- Parentheses are used to show grouping.

The goodie for this lab provides code both to read rules in, and to generate instances of rules.

Reading EBNF

Consider the EBNF specifying US and Canadian postal codes from the text.

```
code:             US-ZIP-code | Can-postal-code
US-zip-code:      main-zip [plus-4]
main-zip:         digit digit digit digit digit
plus-4:           "-" digit digit digit digit
Can-postal-code:  letter digit letter " " digit letter digit
digit:            "0" | "1" | "2" | ... | "9"
letter:           "A" | "B" | "C" | ... | "Z"
```

We could write Scheme code to read EBNF exactly as presented in the text but we would have to read characters. By reformulating the EBNF into a "Scheme-friendly" format we can use (read) directly to read each element of the EBNF. (Changing the input format to suit read is a common approach in Scheme. The disadvantage of doing this versus writing a complete read routine is that error-checking is much harder.)

To represent EBNF for Scheme, we have to change some characters that have special meanings in Scheme to readable characters:

- the "|" character, meaning "or", becomes "!"
- the "[]" characters, meaning that the clause is optional, become "<>"
- the "%" indicates the end of a category
- the symbol *finish* indicates the end of the EBNF rules
- the symbol $ is used to show the beginning of a group and the symbol * is used to show the end of a group
- there is no : after the category name

We also separate the names of EBNF elements from these characters.

We translate the zip code EBNF into Scheme-readable form as:

```
code             US-ZIP-code ! Can-postal-code %
US-zip-code      main-zip < plus-4 > %
main-zip         digit digit digit digit digit %
plus-4           "-" digit digit digit digit %
Can-postal-code  letter digit letter " " digit letter digit %
*finish*
```

Suppose we have the following text in a file named code.ebnf:

```
code             US-ZIP-code ! Can-postal-code %
US-zip-code      main-zip < plus-4 > %
main-zip         digit digit digit digit digit %
plus-4           "-" digit digit digit digit %
Can-postal-code  letter digit letter " " digit letter digit %
*finish*
```

The goodie ebnf.scm provides inrules, a procedure to read EBNF rules. The dialog in Figure 23-1 shows the result of reading the rules using inrules.

PROCEDURE (inrules)

EFFECT   reads EBNF in Scheme-readable form and creates a list structure representing the rules that is usable by gen-ebnf

```
> (with-input-from-file "code.ebnf" (define rules (inrules)))
> rules
((code (us-zip-code) (can-postal-code))
 (us-zip-code (main-zip (*opt* plus-4)))
 (main-zip (digit digit digit digit digit))
 (plus-4 ("-" digit digit digit digit))
 (can-postal-code (letter digit letter digit letter digit)))
```

Figure 23-1   Reading EBNF for postal codes

The goodie provides the following:

- inrules: a procedure to read EBNF rules
- gen-ebnf: a procedure to generate examples from the EBNF rules
- letter: the category of all lowercase alphabetic characters
- digit: the category of the decimal digits 0 through 9
- constant: the category of both letters and digits

Using EBNF to generate strings

An EBNF specification can be thought of as a program for *generating* strings. In this case, we start at a given category and pick random choices from the rules. We keep doing this recursively. The following example shows the generation of random postal/ZIP codes.

```
> (gen-ebnf 'code 5 rules)
b4x 7m9
49099-5436
61282
10629
w2a 3a5
```

This seems like a peculiar thing to want to do, but it is an excellent method for generating test data.

PROCEDURE (gen-ebnf *cat num rules*)
ARGUMENTS
- *cat* is a symbol representing a category in the EBNF
- *num* is the number of examples to generate
- *rules* is the EBNF rule structure to use

EFFECT   prints *num* randomly generated examples using *rules*

The global variable *rep* (in the goodie) specifies the maximum number of repetitions when the EBNF says "0 or more". The cycle of writing rules and generating examples from those rules lets you debug the rules.

Trees in EBNF

The discussion in Chapter 7 presents trees. Figure 23-2 shows a tree and its list representation.

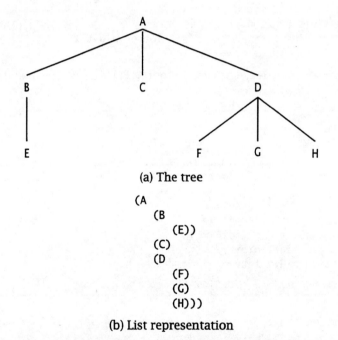

(a) The tree

```
(A
    (B
        (E))
    (C)
    (D
        (F)
        (G)
        (H)))
```

(b) List representation

Figure 23-2   Representing trees as lists

Each node is a list. The value of a node is its car, and its cdr is a list of its descendants. The empty tree is ().
Your problem is to design the EBNF for these trees.

Days of the year

Dates can be specified in EBNF, for example, as part of designing a calendar program. Each date is in the form "YY/MM/DD", for example, "95/06/07". Alternatively, a short form of the date (for the current year) could specify "MM/DD". Then we would like to able to generate a set of dates, followed by "end", as in the following examples.

```
> (gen-ebnf 'dates 5 drules)
47/09/02 63/06/18 end
70/05/02 end
10/07 07/09 end
17/01/04 84/09/26 03/01 end
09/06/11 59/06/19 end
```

BEFORE THE LAB

1. Design the EBNF rules for trees. Is the list (A (B E)) a tree by your rules?
2. Design the EBNF rules for dates. Do your rules permit the date "95/6/7"?

PITFALLS AND ADVICE

You must include spacing in the EBNF, since the code assumes that spacing is important, as in postal codes.

Design your EBNF category by category. You can debug the rules by using gen-ebnf for a particular category, by selecting the category you want using the cat argument.

CHECKPOINT

1. The rules for a floating point number are:

   ```
   float:          ["+" | "-"] integer [ "." integer ]
   integer:        digit {digit}
   ```

   Identify each of the following as valid or invalid, according to the rules for float. For the invalid cases, explain what is incorrect.
   a. 1.13
   b. +.33
   c. -1000
   d. -11.
2. Write EBNF to generate strings composed of an odd number of 2s.
3. Write the EBNF that describes the category zeroes as a Scheme string composed of one or more zeroes.

DURING THE LAB

1. Load the goodie ebnf.scm that provides inrules, a procedure to read EBNF rules.
2. Enter the rules for each of the problems, using inrules. Use gen-ebnf to generate a set of examples specified by your EBNF for trees and dates.

AFTER THE LAB

Chapter 7 shows how the EBNF for the Dream language is directly connected to the interpreter for the language. Part of the problem of interpreting a language is identifying whether a sequence of elements is permitted by the definition of the language.

We can see how the translation from EBNF to a program might proceed. To write a program that determines where a string is a code, the alternatives (for a legal string) are that it is a US-ZIP-code or a Can-postal-code. By following the categories down to the outputs, that is, the occurrences of digit or letter, we can see what to do to recognize a US or Canadian postal code.

Sketch briefly the structure of a program, derived from the EBNF, that would recognize postal codes. What are some of the decisions the program must make? Hint: How can the program determine quickly whether its input is a US or Canadian code?

DELIVERABLES

1. a listing of the EBNF rules (in their Scheme form) for trees and a printout of the examples they generate
2. a listing of the EBNF rules (in their Scheme form) for dates and a printout of the examples they generate
3. the answer to the "After the Lab" question

FOR FURTHER INVESTIGATION

A palindrome is a sentence that reads the same backwards as forwards (see Chapter 3, p. 119), ignoring punctuation, case and blanks, such as "Madam, I'm Adam". In this question we'll consider lists whose elements are either a, b, or c; none of the elements of the lists are themselves lists. An example of a palindromic list is (a b a c a b a).

Write the EBNF that describes all lists containing these elements which are palindromes, i.e., they read the same backwards as forwards.

Deliverables: the EBNF for the palindromes, plus a printout showing that the EBNF rules you have specified generates palindromes

Lab 24
Writing TV Shows

EBNF is a programming language with a specific purpose: defining data (including programs) that has a structure. Many real-life systems have this structure. For example, cartoons often have repetitive plots: much of the humor comes from the inevitability of certain events, such as a coyote falling off a cliff. In this lab, we will see how to use EBNF to generate the plots of cartoons.

WHAT YOU NEED TO KNOW

Read up through Section 7.1. You will have to have completed Lab 23 before attempting this one.

PROBLEM STATEMENT

Many types of books, TV shows, and movies are written according to a formula. In the old *Perry Mason* TV show, the first twenty minutes (including commercials) of each episode was devoted to the murder, the second to the preparation for the trial, and the third to the trial; in the climax of the episode, a person who was not the defendant would break down and admit that he or she had done it.

A writer who works on a show such as this can use some help. A program to help generate the plots would be very useful. This would free the writer to concentrate on detailed dialog (not to mention counting up royalty checks). Since you've just been assigned as the chief writer for the hit new TV series **The Scheme**, you will need a program to manufacture plots for you.

Our solution to this problem uses EBNF. By writing a set of rules, we can define the plot formula. Then gen-ebnf can be used to write the plots.

The plot of *The Scheme* is simple enough. The hero, I. M. Helpless, is a programmer at MegaCorp. A colleague, Joel User, attempts to help I. M. fix bugs. Unfortunately, Joel isn't a very good programmer. The humor of the situation is obvious.[1]

We've written a set of rules for **The Scheme**, shown in Program 24-1. Figure 24-1 shows a demonstration of the program (the output has been slightly reformatted for clarity).

Read these rules and study how they correspond to the plot lines they generate. We want to write a new set of rules, using the same set of EBNF features, to generate TV plots.

More trees

Look back at the representation of trees in Lab 23. We could instead represent leaf nodes simply by their values as shown in Figure 24-2. Each node is a list, except leaf nodes which are represented by the value of the node, whatever it is. An empty tree is (). A tree with root value 1 and two leaves containing 2 and 3 is represented by the list (1 2 3). A tree with root value 1 and two subtrees (2 3) and 4 is represented by the list (1 (2 3) 4).

BEFORE THE LAB

1. Design the EBNF rules for your new cartoon. Make sure that they use a range of EBNF features.
2. Design the EBNF rules for the trees.

---

[1] Hey, *Gilligan's Island* didn't have much of a plot either.

```
saga        setup incident { incident } ending "--- THE END ---" %
setup       "I. M. Helpless asks Joel to help fix his program." %
incident    deletes-all ! improves ! reboots ! config %
deletes-all "Joel clicks on the wrong icon, and accidentally deletes "
            "all of I. M.'s files." %
improves    "In his eagerness to help, Joel grabs the keyboard and "
            "presses a key. The keystroke causes a line to be "
            "deleted from I. M.'s program. Neither Joel nor "
            "I. M. notices this." %
reboots     "Joel finds an undocumented way to reboot I. M.'s computer." %
config      "Joel changes the system configuration in a way that "
            "prevents the machine from booting." %
ending      ending1 ! ending2 %
ending1     "Joel says 'I bet your algorithm is wrong.'" %
ending2     "Joel says 'Hmmm...probably a bug in Scheme.'" %
*finish*
```

Program 24-1   The rules for The Scheme

```
> (define joel
    (with-input-from-file "joeluser.scm"
      (lambda () (inrules))))
> (gen-ebnf 'saga 4 joel)
```
I. M. Helpless asks Joel to help fix his program. Joel changes the
system configuration in a way that prevents the machine from booting.
Joel finds an undocumented way to reboot I. M.'s computer. Joel says
'Hmmm...probably a bug in Scheme.' --- THE END ---

I. M. Helpless asks Joel to help fix his program. Joel finds an
undocumented way to reboot I. M.'s computer. Joel finds an
undocumented way to reboot I. M.'s computer. Joel says 'I bet your
algorithm is wrong.' --- THE END ---

I. M. Helpless asks Joel to help fix his program. In his eagerness to
help, Joel grabs the keyboard and presses a key. The keystroke
causes a line to be deleted from I. M.'s program. Neither Joel nor
I. M. notices this. Joel finds an undocumented way to reboot I. M.'s
computer. Joel says 'I bet your algorithm is wrong.' --- THE END ---

I. M. Helpless asks Joel to help fix his program. Joel finds an
undocumented way to reboot I. M.'s computer. Joel clicks on the wrong
icon, and accidentally deletes all of I. M.'s files. Joel says 'I bet
your algorithm is wrong.' --- THE END ---
```

**Figure 24-1     *The Scheme:* the first four weeks**

## CHECKPOINT

1. The 70s was a decade that brought us many great musical events, including the song "That's the way, uh huh, uh huh, I like it, uh huh, ". The song's lyrics were an endless repetition of the title. Write the EBNF to generate the song, where the base categories are:

```
way "That's the way, " %
huh "uh huh, " %
like "I like it, " %
```

and the start category is song.
```

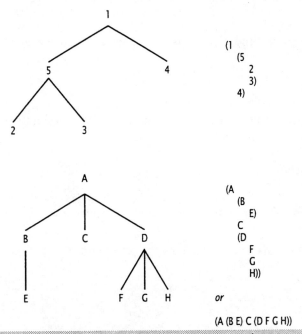

Figure 24-2   Representing trees as lists

2. Write the EBNF that specifies money amounts: $0.25 and $1000.43 are acceptable, but $.24 is not, nor is 2$5.

3. Given the following EBNF that generates "phrases":

```
foo    bar  { baz } bar %
bar    digit ! "-" %
baz    letter ! "." %
*finish*
```

For each of the following phrases, state whether it is a legal phrase according to the EBNF:

    1. 2j4

    2. 24j

    3. -1

DURING THE LAB

1. Type your TV plot rules into a file, and read them with `inrules`.
2. Use `gen-ebnf` to generate a set of examples specified by your EBNF.
3. Type your tree rules into a file, and read them with `inrules`.
4. Use `gen-ebnf` to generate a set of examples specified by your EBNF.

AFTER THE LAB

1. The prime time drama *Silicon Valley* wants a set of EBNF rules. In this series, various characters develop new software and attempt to take over each other's companies. Marriages decay and software release deadlines aren't met. Examine the following rules.

```
story    person action person
person   "bill" | "phillipe" | "gordon" | "lou"
action   " attempts to buy out "
```

One of the limitations of EBNF is that a program such as gen-ebnf has no "memory". It's entirely possible to produce the output bill attempts to buy out bill. Describe a way of changing EBNF to prevent this problem. Hints: the second person is different from the first one in the rule for story; read the code for gen-info carefully; think "alist". You don't have to write any code; just explain how you would do it.

DELIVERABLES

1. listings of your EBNF rules (in their Scheme form) and printouts showing the instances they generate
2. your answer to the "After the Lab" problem

FOR FURTHER INVESTIGATION

A ternary tree is a tree in which a node may have up to three subtrees. Use the tree representation style presented in this lab (leaves are simple the node value). Write EBNF rules for ternary trees, read them in with inrules and generate five examples.

Deliverables: Hand in the EBNF for the ternary trees plus the printout of the generated examples.

Recursive Procedures and Trees

OBJECTIVES

Trees are recursive data structures that can represent ordered collections of elements. Chapter 7 introduces trees. This lab aims to aid your understanding of how recursive procedures operate on trees.

WHAT YOU NEED TO KNOW

Read up through Section 7.2. The material discusses trees, so the procedures we will be writing are tree-recursive. Sections 4.4 and 2.2 in the text discuss various aspects of tree recursion.

PROBLEM STATEMENT

Up to now we've written recursive procedures to handle lists. Lists are first/rest recursive, that is, our procedures process the first element of the list (the car), and then proceed to handle the rest of the list. The car of the list is an element of the list, and may or may not be a list. Whatever it is, it's not at the same "level": it's an element of the list over which we're recursing. The rest, or cdr, of the list is, however, always a list just like the original.

Trees have a different recursive structure. (The discussion here follows Chapter 7. The binary search trees in Chapter 9 are slightly different.) A node stores its own data, its value, and then the list of subtrees. We write tree processing procedures to process all subtrees equally. First, however, before handling the subtrees, we usually must look at the current node. Figure 25-1 shows a tree and its list representation.

The following accessor procedures, value and subtrees, are in the goodie tree.scm. An empty tree is represented by an empty list as in the text. The accessor and predicate procedures are:

```
(define value car)
(define subtrees cdr)
(define empty-tree? null?)
```

The accessors and predicate, the definition of t, and print-node (used later) can be found in the goodie tree.scm.

There are three problems; each section will state the problem and lead you to a solution.

Finding the maximum

The first problem is finding the maximum element in a tree. We'll design a procedure (maximum t) that determines the maximum value in a tree t.

PROCEDURE (maximum *t*)

ARGUMENTS
- *t* is a tree

RETURNS   the maximum element in the tree

What's the recursive step in finding the maximum? An important case is the empty tree. It doesn't make sense to speak of the maximum element of an empty tree, so the procedure should signal an error. What's wrong with returning 0 as the maximum element of an empty tree?

Using 0 as the maximum of an empty tree, we could then write (an incorrect version of) the maximum finder procedure.

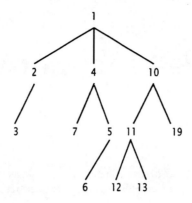

```
(define t
  '(1 (2 (3))
      (4 (7)
         (5 (6)))
      (10 (11 (12) (13))
          (19))))
```

Figure 25-1   A tree and its representation

```
(define wrong-maximum
  (lambda (t)
    (if (empty-tree? t)
      0
      (max (value t)
        (apply max (map wrong-maximum (subtrees t)))))))
```

Under what circumstances would this be the right `maximum` procedure?

The insight that an empty tree has no maximum element tells us a lot about writing `maximum`. We don't want to try to find the maximum of an empty tree. Of course that means we don't return a value for the empty tree. But a consequence of avoiding empty trees is that we must examine the subtrees before recursing, and only apply `maximum` when the subtree is not empty.

Paths and depths

A *path* in a tree is a set of connected nodes, listed in order from the root to a leaf. There are many paths in the tree t, for example, 1-2-3 and 1-4-5-6. We define the *length* of a path in a tree as one less than the number of nodes in the path.

The *depth* of a tree is the length of the longest path in the tree. We can associate a depth with each node in a tree, the depth of the subtree with that node as its root. How would we write a procedure to find the depth of a tree? What's the base case? The depth of an empty tree is not well defined, since there are no nodes.

Is there another base case? When the tree consists of a single node, there is only one path, with one node, with length 0, so the depth of the tree is 0.

What's the recursive step? Depth measures the distance from the root to the farthest leaf. The depth of the leaves in a tree is 0. (We can recognize a leaf node since it has no subtrees.) Here's the recursive step: the depth of a node is one more than the maximum of the depth of its subtrees.

PROCEDURE (depth *t*)

ARGUMENTS
   • *t* is a tree

RETURNS   the depth of the tree, the length of the longest path

---

Printing levels

A *level* in a tree is all nodes at a particular distance from the root, where the *distance* is the length of the path from the root to the node. Level 0 is the root. Level 1 is all nodes directly connected to the root. Consider the problem of printing out a specific level in the tree. The procedure print-node (in the goodie tree.scm) will print a node. We want a procedure (plevel t 1) that prints out all the nodes at level 1 in tree t, as shown in Figure 25-2.

```
> (plevel t 0)
value:1
> (plevel t 1)
value:2
value:4
value:10
> (plevel t 2)
value:3
value:7
value:5
value:11
value:19
> (plevel t 3)
value:6
value:12
value:13
```

Figure 25-2   Printing the values of nodes at a level

How do we go about doing this? If the level we want is 0, we just print the node. If the level is not 0, we can recurse and reduce the level by one.

PROCEDURE (plevel *t* *n*)

ARGUMENTS
   • *t* is a tree

EFFECT   prints level *n* in the tree

BEFORE THE LAB

1. Design maximum and some test inputs. They should vary in the size and structure of the tree as well as the position of the maximum.
2. Translate the description of depth into a recursive procedure to find the depth of a tree. Design its test inputs. What variations in the structure of the tree should be tested?
3. Design plevel and test inputs. The trees should check every condition described in the specification.

PITFALLS AND ADVICE

If you have problems debugging your procedures, write down the box-and-arrow diagrams of the input list and follow the car and cdr operations performed by your list procedure. Use trace to determine the effects of the operations.

CHECKPOINT

1. Is (1 2 3) a tree in our representation? Why or why not?
2. Is ((1) 2 3) a tree in our representation? Why or why not?
3. What is the result of (plevel w 2) where w is:

```
(define w
  '(1 (2 (3))
       (10 (11 (12) (13))
            (19))
       (4 (7)
          (5 (6))))))
```

DURING THE LAB

1. Enter maximum and test it thoroughly.
2. Enter depth and test it thoroughly.
3. Enter plevel and test it thoroughly.

AFTER THE LAB

Assume each node in a tree has k subtrees. How many nodes are there at level d in the tree?

DELIVERABLES

1. the procedures you have written (maximum, depth, and plevel), together with test output for each
2. the answer to the "After the Lab" question

Lab 26
Spreadsheets

In the late 1970s two programmers, Dan Bricklin and Dan Fylstra, invented a new kind of program. Their program, Visicalc, presented a screen that looked like a sheet of accounting paper. The user could enter numbers and formulas into the grid cells, and the program would recalculate the results. Although Visicalc is no longer in use, its successors 1-2-3[1], Excel, and Quattro Pro, are used around the world. In this lab, you will apply your knowledge of evaluators to the task of building a simplified spreadsheet program. By building this program you will strengthen your understanding of evaluators.

WHAT YOU NEED TO KNOW

Read up through Section 7.2. Be sure you understand the Dream evaluator.

PROBLEM STATEMENT

A spreadsheet consists of a set of *expressions* relating some variables. It is fairly easy to change one value and then see how the results change. Thus a manager preparing a budget can ask "What happens to our total costs if I double the research budget and halve the advertising costs?" Seen in this light, spreadsheets are programs in a specialized language. A spreadsheet program such as 1-2-3 is a kind of evaluator.

In this lab, you will write a simple spreadsheet program.

Basic ideas

Your program will use *worksheets*, each of which is a collection of *cells*.[2] Each cell has a name, which is a symbol, and can contain either a number or a formula.

What sort of notation should we use for our formulas? Most of the users of a real program won't know Scheme; in a real system the user types expressions in algebraic notation, e.g., 2+3*4, and the system translates that into the Scheme-like (+ 2 (* 3 4)) inside the program. Conversion between algebraic notation and Scheme notation is beyond the scope of this lab, so we'll stick with a Scheme-like form for expressions.

Real spreadsheets generally have a very sophisticated user interface. A typical spreadsheet allows the user to select and update cells using the mouse, and to produce elaborate graphical presentations based upon the values in the spreadsheet. Our worksheet will be much simpler, and will rely upon the user typing Scheme forms to make things work. This is unacceptable for production software; however, doing things this way will allow us to concentrate upon the important ideas.

The user will create a new worksheet with the Scheme form (sheet 'make). Given a worksheet, the user can use the procedure use-sheet to do calculations using it. use-sheet reads input in the form of commands, as in Figure 26-1. The dialog omits the output of the sheet.

There's nothing to stop a user from keeping multiple worksheets in operation at any one time, as in Figure 26-2.

This means that each worksheet will have its own internal state.

---

[1] 1-2-3 is the program that made the IBM PC successful. Most PC applications were essentially the same as their Apple II or CP/M predecessors; but you had to buy a PC to get 1-2-3. The program was so successful in the mid-1980s that executives referred to their PC's as "1-2-3 machines."

[2] Real spreadsheets organize the cells into a two-dimensional grid, which makes the resulting document look a lot like the kind of documents accountants use. We will be content with a one-dimensional grid, and therefore will use the name *worksheet*, because nothing is spread out.

```
> (define temperatures (sheet 'make))
> (use-sheet temperatures)
sheet> (store celsius (* (- fahrenheit 32) (/ 5 9)))
sheet> (store fahrenheit 32)
sheet> (show)
fahrenheit = 32
celsius = 0
sheet> (store fahrenheit 50)
sheet> (show)
fahrenheit = 50
celsius = 10
sheet> (list)
fahrenheit = 50
celsius = (* (- fahrenheit 32) (/ 5 9))
sheet> (quit)
```

Figure 26-1   A temperature worksheet

```
> (define sheet1 (sheet 'make))
> (define sheet2 (sheet 'make))
> (use-sheet sheet1)
...do some calculations...
(quit)
> (use-sheet sheet2)
...do more calculations...
(quit)
> (use-sheet sheet1)
...and now we're back in the first worksheet again...
```

Figure 26-2   Several worksheets

Worksheet elements

You must write the Scheme procedure:
- (use-sheet *sheet*) reads in commands and carries them out, using the specified worksheet.

The remainder of the lists in the above example are not Scheme forms at all, but merely commands to use-sheet. The following commands are defined:
- (store *cellname expression*) sets the specified cell of the worksheet to the expression in question.
- (show) displays the worksheet, showing the name and numeric value of each cell.
- (list) displays the worksheet, showing the name and expression value of each cell. list and show do the same thing except for showing the values differently.
- (quit) causes use-sheet to terminate (i.e., the recursion terminates).

store, show, list, and quit are not Scheme procedures. Instead, use-sheet reads in commands, each of whom has a car equivalent to one of these symbols.

Each of the items in a worksheet can hold either a number or a list that looks like a Scheme form representing an expression. You must allow addition, subtraction, multiplication, and division.

Recalculation

One of the big questions about real spreadsheet programs is how they recalculate the worksheet. On the surface, this seems quite straightforward: just go to every cell, and re-evaluate the expression. There are two problems with this simple approach:
- A large spreadsheet may have several *thousand* cells. Changing one cell would require that thousands of expressions be re-evaluated, which in turn would make the program too slow to be useful.
- Sometimes a spreadsheet will have **circular dependencies**, in which two cells contain expressions each of which references the other cell. The circularity means that we must recalculate a cell several times. Circular dependencies may seem like the result of a user error, but in fact such circular dependencies

allow the sophisticated spreadsheet user to create iterative computations, similar to our cube root calculations in Chapter 2.

We will finesse this question here, simply recalculating every cell in the worksheet when necessary, and not worrying about circularity. Don't try to do the national budget on our worksheet, though.

Implementing worksheets

Our next concern is how we represent a worksheet in the computer. We will define a `sheet` class with three methods: `(asheet 'get cellname)`, `(asheet 'set! cellname value)`, and `(asheet 'for-each proc)`. Within the class, the easiest way to implement the sheet is as an association list (remember `assv?`). Association lists are easy to program; however, for a large worksheet, association lists would be hopelessly inefficient. On the other hand, they sure are easy to use. We'll use association lists here. Since the `sheet` is a class, it will be easy to change the representation easily later on.

CLASS `sheet`

METHOD `set!` *cellname value*

ARGUMENTS
- *cellname* is the name of a cell
- *value* is any Scheme value

EFFECT   puts the specified value into the cell named *cellname*. If no such cell exists, a new one is created.

METHOD `get` *cellname*

ARGUMENTS
- *cellname* is the name of a cell

RETURNS   the contents of the specified cell of the sheet

METHOD `for-each` *proc*

ARGUMENTS
- *proc* is a procedure that takes two arguments: the name and value of a cell in the worksheet

EFFECT   calls *proc* with the name and value of each cell of the sheet.

Figure 26-3 shows how we can use these methods.

```
> (define mysheet (sheet 'make))
> (mysheet 'set! 'foo 3)
> (mysheet 'set! 'bar '(+ 2 3))
> (mysheet 'get 'bar)
(+ 2 3)
> (mysheet 'for-each
    (lambda (name value)
      (format #t "(~a ~a)~%" name value)))
(foo 3)
(bar (+ 2 3))
```

Figure 26-3   Using sheets

Expressions

How do we evaluate the expressions in our worksheet? We can use the Dream expression evaluator as a template. Expressions are similar to those in Scheme. An expression is one of:
- a number: the value is the number
- a symbol: the value is the value of the cell with that name

- a list: the value is computed recursively. The following list formats are allowed: (+ a b), (- a b), (* a b), (/ a b), with the obvious meanings.

The procedure `evaluate-sheet` will do the work.

PROCEDURE (`evaluate-sheet` *expr sheet*)

ARGUMENTS

- *expr* is a worksheet expression
- *sheet* is the worksheet to be used for cell references

EFFECT   evaluates the expression using current sheet values

BEFORE THE LAB

1. Implement the `sheet` class.
2. Write down some forms to test that the class works correctly. Your tests should include: setting a new cell (one that was not already in the worksheet); setting a cell that already was in the worksheet; getting a value from the worksheet; and displaying the worksheet.
3. Write a procedure `show` that will be used to "show" the worksheet. It will recalculate each cell just before displaying its value. Make sure that you finish off the `evaluate-cell` procedure.
4. Write the "top-level" procedure `use-sheet` that reads in each worksheet command and carries it out. You will probably want each command to be handled by its own "helping" procedure.
5. You are presented with the following problem:

   A computer company's purchases consist of supplies, electronic components, and advertising. The company gets a 10% discount on its components cost. To this total is added local sales tax and federal tax. At present, the sales tax is 11%, and federal tax is 7%, though each of these is likely to change. Compute the total cost to the company, assuming $5000 supplies, $9000 components, and $1000 advertising.

   Prepare a simple worksheet for this problem.

CHECKPOINT

1. We want to store a list of items, starting with nothing, and add or delete elements. Devise a data structure that can support this.
2. What's is the difference between (+ 3 5) and '(+ 3 5)?
3. The `for-each` method used to be called `map`. Is there any reason to have a mapping method for worksheets that returns its a list of results? Why or why not?

DURING THE LAB

1. Type in your worksheet procedures, and try them with the tests you have prepared. Make sure that the procedures work correctly. Produce a printout that demonstrates that they work properly.
2. Try out your `show` procedure. Produce a printout showing that it works correctly.
3. Try `use-sheet`, your top-level procedure, along with the worksheet you prepared for the cost problem. Produce a printout showing that everything works correctly.

AFTER THE LAB

We mentioned at the outset that spreadsheets are evaluators. What do they have in common with the other evaluators systems we studied? Write a short (less than 1 page) report comparing and contrasting spreadsheets with another evaluator.

DELIVERABLES

1. a listing of the `sheet` class, with a printout that shows that they work properly
2. a listing of `evaluate-sheet`
3. a listing of your `show` procedure and a printout showing it works
4. a listing of `use-sheet` and the cost sheet and a printout showing it works for the cost problem
5. your answer to the "After the Lab" question

FOR FURTHER INVESTIGATION

There are many ways of extending your worksheet program. Here are a few suggestions.

1. Obviously, searching a long worksheet to find the value of a cell is extremely time-consuming. Write another version of your `sheet` class using binary search trees (described in Chapter 9) instead of association lists.
2. Modify your recalculation so that you can detect circular references (just generate an error if you find one). We make this problem a bit harder by insisting that you not modify the worksheet itself in the process. Hint: Keep a list of the cells you have visited. On a recursive call, pass the cons of the current cell and the list. You might want to look at the airline routing Case Study at the end of Chapter 4.
3. The top-level of a real spreadsheet program doesn't use commands. Instead, the user directly manipulates the screen. As examples, the user can move from one cell to the next by pressing the up or down arrow keys; the user can replace the contents of a cell by typing over it and pressing ⌈Enter⌉ or ⌈Return⌉. Write a top-level that supports this, if your Scheme system provides the capabilities you will need.

   To solve this problem, you will have to do some research. The Scheme primitive `read-char` reads a single character. You will need to see what character or characters are read when the up or down arrow key is pressed. You will probably need to position the cursor. Not all versions of Scheme support this operation. You might also find the primitive `peek-char` useful.

Deliverables: a program listing and printout for each of the two further investigations

Lab 27
The Self-Evaluator

OBJECTIVES

The purpose of this lab is to give you a chance to explore the self-evaluator. During the lab, you are going to make changes to the evaluator, in order to extend it to support some of the features of full Scheme.

WHAT YOU NEED TO KNOW

Study Chapter 7 carefully, and read over the code for the self-evaluator.

PROBLEM STATEMENT

The self-evaluator in the book just handles Econo-Scheme. Full Scheme is a rich language, with many forms and features not found in Econo-Scheme. By adding features to the self-evaluator, you will not only understand the self-evaluator, but also see that many language features require little work to implement given a good (well-structured) evaluator.

Adding case

Our evaluator doesn't have all of the special forms that Scheme provides. In this problem, you are to add a case form. This turns out to be straightforward: look at the special-forms list, and find out where to add an entry for case. The procedure can be written very simply, using assv. (Remember: each case is a list whose first element is a list whose elements are matched against the test value, and whose cdr is a sequence (hint, hint) of forms to be evaluated.) The symbol else, as well as any symbol that doesn't match any of the cases, should invoke the else case.

Adding while

Pascal programmers sometimes complain that Scheme has no looping statements, such as while and for. We are going to write a while special form that allows you to write code such as:

```
(while (> i 0)
  (format #t "i = ~a~%" i)
  (set! i (sub1 i)))
```

This form will do exactly the same thing as the procedure

```
(define countdown
  (lambda (i)
    (if (> i 0)
      (begin
        (format #t "i = ~a~%" i)
        (countdown (sub1 i))))))
```

A while form essentially does an iteration. Section 7.4 in the text demonstrates a macro that provides while.

We can write a procedure `almost-while`:

```
(define almost-while
  (lambda (test proc)
    (if (test)
      (begin
        (proc)
        (almost-while test proc)))))
```

which is almost right. We would use it as follows:

```
(almost-while
  (lambda () (> i 0))
  (lambda ()
    (format #t "i = ~a~%" i)
    (countdown (sub1 i))))
```

but this is a bit ugly. We'd like a real `while` special form. Once written, it must be added to the special-forms list. The `while` form should return the value of its body, the last time through, or void, if the loop is never done.

Adding `let`

While we're at it, let's add `let`. To do this, you'll need to add a new pair to the `special-forms` list. The procedure will have to evaluate all of the values first, in the current environment, then make a new frame with the variable bindings from the `let`, and then evaluate the `let`-body in this new environment.

Adding `cond`

Chapter 7, p. 380, contains a description of the `cond` form. The `cond` processor in the self-evaluator must work as follows. It processes the list of clauses. If the list is empty, the value is void. If the first element of the first clause is `else`, the following forms are evaluated. If the value of the first element in the first clause is not `#f`, the *exprs* are evaluated. Otherwise the rest of the clause list is evaluated.

Procedures in the evaluator

Our implementation of procedures was as an abstract data type: we defined a procedure in the self-evaluator by a set of procedures that create and access components of procedures. We did this because it allows us to change the representation without changing the rest of the program. (We did this because expert Scheme implementors know extremely efficient ways of storing procedures.) To see whether our goal has been met, we're going to change the procedure representation, in a not-terribly-sensible way.

In this problem, *change only the code in the module* `self-eval-procedure`; you may not change any code other than that.

Our new representation stores procedures as 3-element lists:

- element 1 is the symbol ****procedure****;
- element 2 is the environment;
- element 3 is the lambda form, in the form `(lambda (args) body)` (i.e., in its original form).

This problem should convince you that we made a mistake in the specification (*not* the implementation!) of `make-procedure`. Write a brief paragraph explaining why `make-procedure` should have been designed to take only two arguments, rather than three. (*Don't* make this change here; doing so would require that you change code elsewhere in the evaluator.)

Dynamic scope

[A hard problem] Our evaluator was designed to use static scoping. Older Lisp dialects used **dynamic scoping**, in which a procedure body is evaluated in the environment in which the procedure was *applied*, rather than the one in which it was created. Dynamic scope allows us to do some things that static scope doesn't:

```
dyneval> ; This is a dialog with an evaluator for a
dyneval> ; dynamically-scoped version of Scheme.
dyneval> (define foo (lambda (x) (+ x y)))
dyneval> ((lambda (y) (foo 12)) 17)
```

29

As you can see, with dynamic scoping, we can rebind a variable and have that binding take effect in procedure calls.

We want to modify `self-application` to do dynamic rather than static scoping (Hint: You only have to change one line of this procedure.)

Scheme doesn't have dynamic scoping in this sense, but many Scheme implementations provide **fluid binding**, which provides many of the benefits of dynamic scoping.

Global tracing

It's possible to get the self-evaluator to print out the name and arguments of a procedure at every application. You can write the procedure `(global-trace flg)` that sets a flag in the evaluator. If true, every time a procedure is called, a line is written out with the name of the procedure and its arguments.

The hard part is to display the procedure's name, not its value. Unnamed procedures can be displayed as `*anonymous-lambda*`.

Single stepping

We could also require the evaluator to print a trace for each application and then stop. Global tracing is fine if there are only a few applications in the computation we are tracing. **Stepping** through a program means printing a trace at each step and stopping, to consider the result. You will need to extend the change you made for tracing to accept input: the user can type the number of further applications before the next stop. For example, if the evaluator reads 0 after stopping, it stops after the next application. Inputting 4 means perform five more applications before stopping. A negative number means continue without stopping.

Implementing this should be straightforward: by requesting input, the program automatically stops.

BEFORE THE LAB

For each of the problems, design the appropriate addition to the evaluator and prepare a dialog with the evaluator that demonstrates that you have made the change correctly.

PITFALLS AND ADVICE

1. This lab involves a small amount of code that must be added to a large program. To be successful, you must be sure you have studied the description of the self-evaluator in the book.
2. Work on each of the following problems *before* going to the lab. If you get stuck on any one problem, try the others.
3. You will probably be hesitant to start working on this lab until you understand everything. That won't work: the whole point of this lab is to understand the self-evaluator by making modifications to it. Attempting to understand the self-evaluator while seated at the computer is unlikely to provide enlightenment.
4. The semantics of `let` is tricky. Make sure that you are implementing `let` and not `let*`.

CHECKPOINT

1. What is the major difference between Dream and the self-evaluator?
2. What is the major difference between the clauses in a `case` form and the clauses in a `cond` form?
3. What standard Scheme data structure is used in the self-evaluator to represent the bindings of names to values?

DURING THE LAB

The evaluator is in a goodie named `selfeval.scm`. To start the self-evaluator, load the goodie, and type `(top-level)`. To exit the self-evaluator, type `(stop)`.

1. Type in the code that handles `case`, `while`, `let`, and `cond`. For each new evaluator feature, run the self-evaluator with the new feature and show that it works.
2. Try both the statically and dynamically scoped versions of the evaluator with the `foo` example. Try them both with the following, as well:

```
(define twice (lambda (f) (lambda (x) (f (f x)))))
((twice add1) 2)
```

You will see that the modified evaluator doesn't know about the binding for f here.

3. Add global tracing and demonstrate it working.
4. Add single stepping and demonstrate it working, using a variety of inputs.

AFTER THE LAB

1. let is a form of lambda, yet when it came time to implement it, we didn't actually convert the let form into a lambda application. There are good reasons for not doing this conversion (it's more efficient not to). Why was it a good idea to explain let in terms of lambda? What does this tell you about the relationship between the language specification and the evaluator?

2. John and Jane are working together on a big program. John writes

```
(define get-data
  (lambda ()
    (let ((metric? #t))
      (if metric?
        ...)
      ...
      (process-data)
      ...)))
```

Jane writes

```
(define metric?
  (lambda (x)
    (eqv? (cdr x) 'kilometres)))
(define process-data
  (lambda ()
    (let ((y ...))
      (if (metric? y)
        ...))))
```

a. What happens when John and Jane load their code into Scheme? Does an error occur?
b. Suppose John and Jane load their code into the evaluator for a dynamically scoped language whose syntax is the same as Scheme. What happens? Does an error occur?
c. What can you conclude about the value of dynamic scoping when writing a large program?

DELIVERABLES

1. One listing of your revised evaluator, in response to the first three problems (don't include the revision needed to support dynamic scoping). All changes you have made must be clearly identified with a comment giving your name and a detailed description of the change (saying "This is a solution to problem 2" is not enough; your comment must explain *what* you have changed, and *why* you needed to change it to solve the problem). Markers would appreciate it if you would highlight (with a yellow pen) all places where you made changes.

2. a listing of the change you made to self-application in order to implement dynamic scoping

3. execution runs (dialogs with your evaluator) that demonstrate that the changes you have made do indeed solve the problems they were intended to

4. a listing of the change to the evaluator to add global tracing, together with a listing showing it working

5. a listing of the change to the evaluator to add single stepping, together with a listing showing it working

6. the explanatory paragraph on procedures

7. the answer to the "After the Lab" question

Lab 28
Tables

Tables are important tools in organizing information. Relation operators provide a rich language, embedded in Scheme by DBScheme, to express organiztation.

WHAT YOU NEED TO KNOW

Read the text through the end of Section 8.4. Make sure you understand tables.

PROBLEM STATEMENT

You've begun work at Boing-Boing corp who have recently begun developing the successor to the highly-touted 555 aircraft. They need you to set up the database of parts for the machine. There are several type of information they have: information on parts, suppliers, costs, supplier's addresses, and which parts contain which other parts. Your job is to organize the data using DBScheme. Here's the information you get:

"Aardvark Corp., at 100 Cut-rate Ave., and Zebra Ltd., at 001 Basic Drive, supply the AB123 part, which contains 4 ZY001 and 3 UV988 parts. Aardvark charges $0.99 for each AB123, while Zebra charges $1.23. Zebra supplies the ZY001 for $0.50 each. Lameco, at 909 Mellon Way, supplies the UV988 for $1.99 each, while Aadvark supplies the UV988 for $1.80.

Each ZY001 contains 3 ST009 parts, available from Zebra at $4.50. Each ST009 contains 2 UV988s."

We will want to find the suppliers of a part, the address of the part. In fact, we will want to access all information about parts, suppliers, and costs. To use the DB, we will need to perform a range of queries.

Here's the set of queries we'll answer:

1. Which companies supply part UV988?

2. How many UV988s does AB123 contain?

3. Which parts does AB123 contain?

Besides answering the obvious queries about the information directly entered in the database, we might want to answer queries such as "what parts does AB123 contain?" The database should contain information about the parts *directly* contained by AB123, but this query asks for even those parts that are indirectly contained. This is a recursive question that is beyound the direct capability of the relational operators. For this query we'll need to write a procedure that uses `table-for-each-row`, the DBScheme analog of `for-each`. (The organization tree in Chapter 7 is similar to the containment relation. Review the procedures that work on trees for hints on how to solve this problem.)

We'll need to find all the parts directly contained in AB123, and then for each of them find the parts they contain. To avoid duplication, we must check whether a part is new or already appears on the list of parts. For all new parts, we repeat the process of searching the table that represents the containment relation, and then using `table-for-each-row` on all rows that contain information about the part in question.

BEFORE THE LAB

1. Write a "shoebox" table for the data needed in this problem.
2. Normalize these tables into 3NF. There should be at least three tables.
3. Write out the DBScheme forms that express the tables as you have written them in 3NF.
4. Write out DBScheme queries that answer the three questions given above.
5. Write the DBScheme forms that generate the recursive query `contains`.

CHECKPOINT

1. Do DBScheme forms commute, that is, does rearranging them (putting the inside one on the outside) change the meaning of the query?
2. Could the recursive procedure for computing `contains` run into an infinite loop? What structure of the tables would cause `contains` to do so? Would our current table cause an infinite loop?
3. What requirement is needed for a table to be in Second Normal Form?

DURING THE LAB

1. Load the goodie `dbscheme.scm` and create the tables you have designed.
2. Run the three DBScheme queries and get their answers.
3. Enter your recursive procedure for computing `contains` and find out what parts `AB123` contains.

AFTER THE LAB

1. We could organize the database so that there is no need for a recursive query to determine where a part contains another. How would we do that?

DELIVERABLES

1. listings of your DBScheme tables to represent the database
2. your DBscheme forms to answer the queries and the printout to show that they work properly
3. your `contains` procedure and a printout showing that it works
4. your answers to the "After the Lab" questions

FOR FURTHER INVESTIGATION

Often we use the form:

```
(table-print
  (table-project
     atable '(acolumn)) compare-proc 'acolumn)
```

We'd rather just say:

```
(table-print-column atable 'acolumn)
```

What information would our tables need to allow use to implement `table-print-column`? Put that information into the table module and alter `make-table` so that you can enter the information when you create a table.

Implement `table-print-column`.

Deliverables: a listing of the part of the `table` module you changed and a listing of `table-print-column` and printout showing that it works

Lab 29

Measuring Algorithm Complexity

Up to this point, we have determined the cost of a procedure by counting (by hand) calls to procedures, and deriving a formula from the results. Software tools let us capture the number of procedure calls automatically. This lab shows how to use objects to build tools to count procedure calls.

In this lab, we're going to investigate insertion sort and Quicksort.

WHAT YOU NEED TO KNOW

Make sure you have read up through Section 9.3.

PROBLEM STATEMENT

The way to count procedure calls is to use *meters*. A meter is a procedure, along with some apparatus to count calls and report results.

To see how meters are used, let's go back to mult%1 and mult%2 in Chapter 2, shown in Program 29-1.

```
(define mult%1
  (lambda (a b)
    (if (= b 0)
        0
        (m:+ a (mult%1 a (sub1 b))))))
(define mult%2
  (lambda (a b)
    (if (= b 1)
        a
        (m:+ (mult%2 (double a) (halve b))
             (if (not (even? b)) a 0)))))
```
Program 29-1   Metered multiplication procedures

In those procedures, the operation that seems to take time is + (you might also think that double, halve, add1 and sub1 are time-consuming, but they're not: most computers can execute these specialized addition and multiplication primitives very quickly). We can make an addition meter. meter+ is the the *meter* (an object that counts the number of calls), and m:+ is the *metered procedure* (a procedure that carries out the tasks that the original procedure was supposed to do), shown in Figure 29-1.

```
> (define meter+ (meter 'make +))
> (define m:+ (meter+ 'proc))
> (meter+ 'count)
0
> (m:+ 2 3)
5
> (meter+ 'count)
1
```
Figure 29-1   Metering plus

```
> (meter+ 'reset)
> (mult%1 3871 2397)
9278787
> (meter+ 'count)
2397
> ; Now let's try the second version.
> (meter+ 'reset)
> (mult%2 3871 2397)
9278787
> (meter+ 'count)
11
```

Figure 29-2   Metering multiplication procedures

We will give meters names such as `meter-double` (a meter for procedure `double`); the corresponding metered procedure will be named `m:double` (the colon is a valid character in a name). Figure 29-2 shows some data on these procedures.

As you can see, `mult%1` required 2397 additions to compute its result; `mult%2` only required 11. Even though each repetition of `mult%2` takes longer, there are far fewer of them, and therefore we can safely conclude that `mult%2` is much faster than `mult%1`.

Program 29-2 shows the definition of the `meter` class.

```
(define-class meter
 (constructor proc)
 (slots (count 0))
 (methods (message)
  ((proc)
   (lambda x
     (set! count (add1 count))
     (apply proc x)))
  ((reset)
   (set! count 0))
  ((count) count)))
```

Program 29-2   meter

CLASS meter

METHOD make *proc*
  • *proc* is a procedure
RETURNS   a meter for *proc*

METHOD proc
RETURNS   a metered procedure for *proc*

METHOD reset
EFFECT   sets the count to 0

METHOD count
RETURNS   the number of calls to the metered procedure since the last *reset*

Only the code for `proc` uses any special Scheme features. First, the procedure is variadic (accepts any number of arguments): this is shown by writing a single argument name, rather than a list of arguments, after lambda. Second, the procedure uses the Scheme primitive apply, which applies its procedure to a list of arguments; thus (apply + '(2 3)) ⇒ 5.

Application to sorting

The most significant cost in sorting is the time needed to compare elements. If we measure the number of comparisons made, we can get a pretty good idea of the amount of work being done. We'll use insertion sort, as shown in Program 29-3. Insertion sort produces the results shown in Figure 29-3.

```
(define insertion-sort
  (lambda (lst less)
    (insertion-sort-h lst less '())))
(define insertion-sort-h
  (lambda (lst less res)
    (if (null? lst)
        res
        (insertion-sort-h (cdr lst)
          less
          (insert-in-order (car lst) res less)))))
(define insert-in-order
  (lambda (item lst less)
    (if (null? lst)
      (cons item '())
      (if (less item (car lst))
        (cons item lst)
        (cons (car lst)
          (insert-in-order item (cdr lst) less))))))
```

Program 29-3   Sort procedure using insertion

```
> (define meter< (meter 'make <))
> (define m:< (meter< 'proc))
> (insertion-sort '(13 22 19 8) m:<)
(8 13 19 22)
> (meter< 'count)
4
> (meter< 'reset)
> (insertion-sort '(13 65 19 44 22 37 19 8 51 29 90) m:<)
(8 13 19 19 22 29 37 44 51 65 90)
> (meter< 'count)
41
```

Figure 29-3   Metering insertion sort

Going from 4 elements to 11 resulted in a ten-fold increase in the number of comparisons. $O(...)$ notation tells us what happens when n, the number of elements in the list, gets large. Clearly, typing in a huge number of values is tedious. Instead, we can use a procedure to construct a random list of data using random numbers:

```
(define make-random-list
  (lambda (n max)
    (if (= n 0)
      '()
      (cons (random max)
        (make-random-list (sub1 n) max)))))
```

This procedure returns a list of n items, each a random number between 0 and max−1. We can use this list as an argument to a sorting procedure, and meter the number of comparisons. The results are pretty frightening: sorting one random list of 1000 elements, using insertion sort, required 248026 comparisons; another list required 246550 comparisons.

BEFORE THE LAB

1. The first step is to get familiar with meters and metered procedures. Suppose we create a metered procedure for multiplication:

```
> (define meter* (meter 'make *))
> (define m:* (meter* 'proc))
> (m:* 3 5)
15
> (meter* 'count)
1
```

   Draw a snapshot at the time we multiply 3 by 5 (i.e., at the time we evaluate (apply * '(3 5)).

2. We could tabulate the length of list versus the number of comparisons, but when the list length gets past about 20, tables become hard to understand. A graph is just the thing here: however, since we are going to compare two sorting algorithms, we have to be careful how we go about gathering data. Simply generating two different sets of lists won't work, because it doesn't mean much to compare the performance of algorithm A sorting list α with that of algorithm B sorting list β.

   As a first step, write a procedure generate-random-lists that generates random lists (with elements between 0 and a million) of a specified set of lengths; thus, for example,

```
> (generate-random-lists '(1 2 3))
((70585) (70511 22529) (47717 45633 75881))
```

   This is a one-liner if you use map!

3. We need a procedure number-of-comparisons, shown in Figure 29-4. Write it. You will use it as follows:

```
> (number-of-comparisons (generate-random-lists '(100 200 300))
    insertion-sort <)
(2407 10932 21655)
```

   number-of-comparisons must create a metered comparison procedure from its third argument. Once you have done that, this too is a simple use of map.

4. Write a procedure (based upon the graph code you wrote for previous labs) that graphs the length of the list against the number of comparisons required, e.g.,

```
> (let ((lengths '(100 200 300)))
    (let ((lists
            (generate-random-lists lengths)))
      (graph lengths
        (number-of-comparisons
          lists
          insertion-sort
          <))))
```

   Given the large number of comparisons that will be done in some cases, you'll need to have the option of log-scaling the y axis (i.e., the y values will be the logarithms of the corresponding values). This can either be done by having two separate plotting procedures, or, better, by passing a y-scaling argument to the plotting procedure.

5. You will also need a procedure that produces a list of numbers from n down to 1, e.g.,

```
> (make-sorted-list 15)
(15 14 13 12 11 10 9 8 7 6 5 4 3 2 1)
```

PROCEDURE (number-of-comparisons *lists sorter compare*)

ARGUMENTS
- *lists* is the result of generate-random-lists
- *sorter* is a sorting procedure
- *lists* is a comparison procedure

RETURNS   a list consisting of the number of comparisons for each of the input lists

Figure 29-4   The number-of-comparisons procedure

CHECKPOINT

1. map and for-each differ in two significant ways. What are they?

2. Suppose oddsort (a hypothetical sorting algorithm) has its worst case when the first half of the data are sorted in ascending order and the second half in descending order. In practice, do you think that this case would be as likely to occur as sorted input in ascending order or descending order? Which of the three cases seems most likely?

3. Why do we give number-of-comparisons an unmetered procedure as its input, instead of a metered procedure?

DURING THE LAB

1. All of the code is in the goodie sortcode.scm. Load it, and take a look through it.

2. Define a metered addition procedure named m:+, and make sure that it works with mult%1. Find out how many additions are needed to multiply 19 by 37.

3. Find out how large a list you want to work with. Experiment with lists of length 100, 150, and so on, until you get to a length where you have to wait 30 seconds or so for the sorting to finish. Needless to say, don't display the output; it will produce far too much output! We claim that these sorting procedures work; you don't have to verify that. One way to avoid seeing the output is to use begin:

```
(begin
    (insertion-sort ...)
    'ok)
```

which simply displays ok at the end.

4. Prepare a form that generates a set of lists; your set should have about 20 elements, with lengths ranging from 1 to the maximum tolerable value *in regular steps*; if the maximum is 2000, it should take 30 seconds to sort it. Sorting 20 lists may take up to 10 minutes. The lists should appear in ascending order sorted by size, and in regular steps of size—THIS IS IMPORTANT for the graphs you will produce later. Keep the list of test sizes (sorted) and the test lists around for later use.

5. Using number-of-comparisons, get a list of the number of comparisons to sort each of these lists with insertion sort. Graph the results.

6. Now, *using the same set of lists* (do *not* produce new ones), do the same thing with Quicksort (you do not need to understand how Quicksort works in order to do this). You call quicksort with a comparison procedure:

```
(number-of-comparisons
            lists
            quicksort
            compare-integers)
```

(The procedure compare-integers is provided with the goodie.) You may have to vary the scaling to get a good graph. It would be nice to produce a graph with the data for both insertion sort and Quicksort overlaid (in this case, the scaling may be a bit funny), but this is hard. You can do it if you wish, but for our purposes here, just describe how the two graphs differ.

7. Now, instead of using random data, use the sorted lists you got from make-sorted-list. Use lists of the same lengths you used with the random data, and again produce separate graphs of each, along with a graph showing results for both.

8. Finally, consider the procedure

```
(define mystery
  (lambda (m n)
    (if (= m 0)
        '()
        (m:cons m
          (if (= n 0)
              (mystery (sub1 m) m)
              (mystery m (sub1 n)))))))))
```

Without trying to analyze this procedure, produce a graph of the number of calls to cons (hence the metered name m:cons) performed in evaluating (mystery n n).

AFTER THE LAB

1. Look over your graphs. You should have obtained substantially different results from the random and sorted data tests. Write a brief explanation (using the code for the procedure) of why insertion sort is so fast on data that is already in (reverse) order.

2. Using $O(\dots)$ notation, derive a formula for the number of calls to cons in (mystery n n).

3. cons is an interesting procedure. Since each time we call cons we get a new pair, and since each pair takes up memory, the use of cons imposes a space charge. Assuming that our machine has 1 million bytes of memory, and each pair takes up 16 bytes (a typical figure for many Scheme systems), how large a value of n can we use in (mystery n n)? (If you know about virtual memory, ignore it for this question.)

DELIVERABLES

1. a listing of m:+, the session showing it working with mult%1 and the number of additions in multiplying 19 by 37

2. the list of sizes for the random lists you generate, the number of comparisons used in insertion sort (for random lists), and the graph of these numbers

3. the number of comparisons used in Quicksort (for random lists), and the graph of these numbers

4. the numbers and graphs for insertion sort and Quicksort on sorted lists

5. the graph of the number of conses used by mystery

6. the answers to the "After the Lab" questions

Lab 30

A Mathematics Assistant

People are often surprised that good programmers don't write every program from scratch, but attempt to reuse code from previous projects.

In this lab, you will get some experience writing a somewhat larger program than you have heretofore attempted. This lab builds on the mathematical visualization lab, the spreadsheet lab, and the symbolic differentiation goodie, `deriv.scm`.

Read up through Section 10.2. Make sure you understand pattern matching and the `match?` procedure.

For this lab, you will do much of the work outside the lab. Plan your work carefully, so that when you go into the lab you know exactly what you are doing.

Also, **start early**. You will need several sessions at the computer to finish this project. Prepare much of your code in advance of your first lab session, so that you will be able to ask your questions where necessary.

The remainder of this lab describes what you are to do. A section at the end describes what is to be handed in.

This lab is not structured as our other labs are. Rather than us telling you what to do at each step, you must make a plan for your work.

The problem

In these labs, together with the text, we have written a large amount of code that deals with mathematical functions. In the book we saw procedures for finding zeroes and derivatives, and for graphing. None of these procedures was written as part of a larger project, but merely to illustrate some particular point.

In this project, we are going to develop a software package that allows users to do various types of mathematical analyses. A user will be able to type in a formula, to graph it, and to find a root or roots near a specified value. Users will be able to store their formulas on files, and reload them subsequently, so that they can continue an analysis over several sessions.

Functions will be written in a Scheme-like notation, allowing the operators +, -, *, /, and ^, the latter referring to exponentiation (only integer constant powers will be allowed here). This is basically the same notation used in the spreadsheet lab.

An example dialog with the program appears in Figure 30-1. The first line is a Scheme form that starts the assistant. Your program then reads commands (in a list format, as with the spreadsheet lab) until it gets a `stop` command. In order to know whether you're talking to your program or to Scheme, your program should display a prompt before reading a command.

In this example, we first defined a formula named `square`. We asked for the derivative of `square` (implicitly with respect to x). We then asked for `square` to be graphed over the range from 0 to 10. Next, we exercised the root-finding capability of the program: we asked first for a root of the function $x^2 - 4$ in the range from 1.5 to 2.5, with epsilon 0.001; next, for a root of `square` (x^2) between -1 and +1 with the same epsilon; and, finally, for a root of `square-9` ($x^2 - 9$) between 0 and 10, with epsilon 0.001. Finally, we saved our formulas (only `square` in this example), and exited.

Formulas in the Mathematics Assistant look much as they did in the spreadsheet lab. Scheme syntax (parentheses around each expression and subexpression, operator first) is used, even though most mathematicians would be happier with normal algebraic notation.

```
> (mathematics-assistant)
Mathematics assistant ready...your wish is my command!
ma> (formula square (* x x))
square
ma> (derivative square)
(+ (* x 1) (* x 1))
ma> (graph square 0 10)
ma> (find-zero (- (* x x) 4) 1.5 2.5 0.001)
2.0
ma> (find-zero square -1.0 1.0 0.001)
0.0
ma> (find-zero (- square 9) 0 10 0.001)
3.0
ma> (save "myformulas.math")
Saving square
ma> (stop)
...and a pleasant day to you!
```

Figure 30-1   Using the math assistant

- the only variable is x; all other names are either constants or the names of other formulas.
- when a formula contains the name of another formula within it, the named formula is substituted for the name. Thus, for example, if square is as defined above, then (- square 5) and (- (* x x) 5) are exactly the same.

Symbolic Differentiation

The goodie deriv.scm contains a procedure derivative that uses pattern matching to compute the derivative of a formula.

PROCEDURE (derivative *formula variable*)

ARGUMENTS
- *formula* is a formula
- *sorter* is a variable

RETURNS   a new formula that is the derivative of *formula*

Rules describe the relation between a formula and its derivative. The rules of calculus include:

$$\frac{d(u+v)}{dx} = \frac{du}{dx} + \frac{dv}{dx} \qquad \text{(sum rule)}$$

$$\frac{d(uv)}{dx} = u\frac{dv}{dx} + v\frac{du}{dx} \qquad \text{(product rule)}$$

Our differentiator should work as follows:

```
> (derivative '(+ x 2) 'x)
(+ 1 0)
```

This says that $\frac{d(x+2)}{dx} = 1 + 0$; a smart program would simplify this to 1, but we'll leave that part as an exercise for you.

The program should probably "reason" as follows:

$$\frac{d(x+2)}{dx} = \frac{dx}{dx} + \frac{d2}{dx} = 1 + 0$$

It has used the sum rule once here, but in a more complex example, such as

```
> (derivative '(+ (* 2 x) (- x)) 'x)
(+ (+ (* 2 1) (* x 0)) (- 1))
```

it must use the product rule once and the sum rule several times. This example demonstrates the need for a simplifier. The reasoning here is a bit more complicated:

$$\frac{d(2x-x)}{dx} = \frac{d(2x)}{dx} - \frac{dx}{dx} = (2\frac{dx}{dx} - x\frac{d2}{dx}) - \frac{dx}{dx} = (2 \times 1 - 1 \times 0) - 1 = 1$$

Each = in these steps corresponds to a deduction performed by the differentiator.

The differentiator uses rules written as lists. The product rule looks like this:

```
(
    (* (u) (v))
    (+ (* (u) (d v)) (* (v) (d u))))
```

This rule is a list with two elements. The first is a *pattern* to be matched, and the second is the replacement value. In a pattern, a wild card (corresponding to ? in QScheme) is shown as a list containing a symbol. For example, matching (* (+ x 2) x) against this pattern pairs the symbol u with (+ x 2) and the symbol v with x.

The replacement value uses the same system, but the lists can be a bit more complicated: a list that consists of (d *symbol*) is replaced with the derivative of the pattern that matched *symbol*. This is essentially a recursive call to the differentiator. Thus in our above example, (v) would be replaced with x, but (d v) would be (recursively) replaced with 1.

Here's the rules we'll use in our differentiator:

```
(define differentiation-rules
  '( ((+ (u) (v)) (+ (d u) (d v)))
     ((- (u))     (- (d u)))
     ((- (u) (v)) (- (d u) (d v)))
     ((* (u) (v)) (+ (* (u) (d v)) (* (v) (d u))))
     ((/ (u) (v)) (/ (- (* (u) (d v)) (* (v) (d u))) (* (v) (v))))
     ((^ (u) (k)) (* (k) (* (d u) (^ (u) (- (k) 1)))))))
```

Implementing the differentiator Let's start with the matching itself. Suppose we match (+ (* 2 x) x) with (+ (u) (v)).

```
> (match '(+ (* 2 x) x) '((+ (u) (v)) (+ (d u) (d v))))
((((u) * 2 x) ((v) . x)) (+ (d u) (d v)))
```

match is similar to var-match? presented in Chapter 10. It expects a rule as its second argument, whose car is matched against the first argument. Its output will be a list of two elements: an alist matching the variables from the left-hand side of the rule to elements from the target, and the replacement value from the right-hand side of the rule. match returns the empty list if the patterns do not match.

match is responsible for seeing whether a formula matches the pattern of a particular rule. find-match is responsible for scanning through the entire set of rules and determining which rule is applicable.

```
(define find-match
  (lambda (formula rules)
    (if (null? rules)
        (error 'find-match "Can't find applicable rule")
        (let ((result (match formula (car rules))))
          (if (null? result)
              (find-match formula (cdr rules))
              result)))))
```

The output of find-match is a list of two parts: the car is the bindings from the match, and the cdr is the replacement of the successful rule. (Note that there will *always* be a successful rule; if no rule applies, the system can't differentiate the formula, and reports an error.)

```
> (find-match '(+ x (* x 3))
                     differentiation-rules)
((((u) . x) ((v) * x 3)) (+ (d u) (d v)))
```

find-match, then, tells us everything we need to know: the bindings from the original expression, and a "template" for building the derivative. All we need to do is to put everything together.

The main procedure of the differentiator is `derivative`, which takes a formula and a variable of differentiation as arguments, as shown in Program 30-1.

```
(define derivative
  (lambda (formula variable)
    (if (atom? formula)
      (if (eqv? formula variable) 1 0)
      (let*
        ((result (find-match formula differentiation-rules))
         (subparts (car result))
         (derivatives
           (map
             (lambda (part)
               (cons (list 'd (car (car part)))
                 (derivative (cdr part) variable)))
             subparts))
         (bindings (append derivatives subparts))
         (pattern-elements (map car bindings))
         (pattern-replacements (map cdr bindings))
         (new-formula (car (cdr result))))
        (for-each
          (lambda (old new)
            (set! new-formula (subst new old new-formula)))
          pattern-elements
          pattern-replacements)
        new-formula)))))
```

Program 30-1   The derivative procedure

For us, the variable of differentiation will be *x*, and therefore the argument will be `'x`. However, allowing the variable to be an argument allows us to do partial derivatives, should we be so inclined. There are two major cases.

- symbols other than the one we're differentiating with respect to and numbers have derivative 0; the variable of differentiation has derivative 1.
- any other formula will have to be a list, either a sum or product, which breaks into parts; we must differentiate each part of the formula via a recursive call.

`derivative` constructs a master list of bindings for replacement. For each wild-card name such as (u), it adds to the bindings a corresponding entry for (d u). The bindings list for the above example is:

```
(
  ((d u) . 1)
  ((d v) + (* x 0) (* 3 1))
  ((u) . x)
  ((v) * x 3)
)
```

All that remains is to do the substitution. We use `subst`; because we will have many bindings, we can map down the list of bindings, substituting in turn for each binding.

It's possible to write a differentiator in which the rule are replaced by a large number of `if`-forms. The resulting program isn't readable or extensible, but it will work.

Simplification and integration

There are many problems in mathematics that are similar to differentiation in that we want a formula or equation as our answer instead of a number. We have already mentioned simplification: there are a large number of operations that simplify formulae. Consider, for example, the formula

$$2x^2 + 3x(x + 1) - 4 * \sin 0 = 2x^2 + 3x^2 + 3x - 4 \times 0 = 5x^2 + 3x$$

We can set up a set of rules for simplification (e.g., $1x = x$, $0x = 0$, $x - x = 0$) and then keep applying them until the formula can't be simplified any further. This method often doesn't work, because we might get trapped in an infinite loop. In algebra, sometimes it makes sense to expand an expression $(a(b + c) = ab + ac)$, and sometimes it makes sense to factor an expression $(ab + ac = a(b + c))$. No rule has ever been found which would allow complete automatic simplification. Real mathematics systems generally expect the user to specify when expansion and factoring are to be done.

Commands your program must understand

This program, as with the worksheet program for Lab 26, is command-driven. Your program displays a prompt, and then reads a command. The following commands are defined:

- (clear)
  Forget all formulas that are currently known. After executing a clear command (and at the beginning of execution), the only name that will be known will be pi.
- (derivative *formula*)
  Find the derivative of *formula* with respect to x.
- (evaluate *formula* *value*)
  Evaluate *formula* with x equal to value.
- (find-zero *formula* *low* *high* *epsilon*)
  Find a root of *formula* between x=*low* and x=*high* to accuracy *epsilon*. The program complains if no root exists in that range; if more than one root exists, then which one the program returns is unpredictable.
- (formula *name* *formula*)
  Bind the name *name* to the value *formula*.
- (graph *formula* *low* *high*)
  Draw a graph of *formula* in the range from *low* to *high*.
- (load *filename*)
  Load formulas from the specified file. These formulas are added to any that are currently known.
- (save *filename*)
  Save all formulas in the specified file. Write out each formula as a separate list.
- (stop)
  mathematics-assistant quits.

Error checking

This program is intended to be used by humans. Humans make mistakes. Your program must therefore behave in an appropriate manner, regardless of what the user throws at it.

Scheme allows extremely elaborate error trapping. We won't get into that; therefore, there may be errors (e.g., invalid characters in the input, or division by zero) that will crash the program. However, your program should detect at least the following errors:

- invalid commands;
- formulas with invalid operators (e.g., (foo 3 4));
- formulas with the wrong number of operands (e.g., (+ 2 3 4)).

In general, when you detect an error, you should produce an informative message, and then abandon processing the command. Be careful to make your message informative.

PITFALLS AND ADVICE

This project is large enough that you will have to break it down into pieces to get it working. Remember that much of the code already exists, in examples and goodies, or in labs you've done already.

Hints on program design and implementation

As mentioned earlier, this is a complex programming task. Although you have done many of the pieces before, putting them together isn't as easy as you might think. In particular, starting on some small piece of the task won't necessarily help you.

The best thing to do is to plan out your design on paper. Start with your main procedure, mathematical-assistant, and then identify various subtasks to be carried out. Each command, obviously, should correspond to a procedure; try to identify, for each such procedure, a set of steps to be carried out. Look for common subtasks (e.g., checking a formula for errors).

Do this analysis in a top-down manner: draw a tree structure with your main program as the root, the various major procedures (called by the root procedure) below that, and the subprocedures below that (there may be four or five levels before you're finished). Actually, your diagram won't be a tree, because there will be procedures that are called from many places.

Remember the Rule of 7 ± 2: if a procedure is longer than about 10 lines, it is too long to understand, and should be broken into sub-procedures. (Of course, if a procedure contains helpers, we don't include them in the count.)

Once you have completed your plan, go on a "raiding" expedition. Find code, either from goodies or from previous labs, that might be useful. Naturally, since these various pieces weren't designed to work together, you will have to study each in order to see whether it must be modified to work with the other pieces.

Don't start by writing all the error-check code. Get the framework working first, and only then go back to put in the error-checking. One very good way of doing this is to make **stubs**, or dummy procedures, e.g.,

```
(define is-formula-ok?
  (lambda (formula)
    #t)))
```

and only go back to put in the real error checking later on.

Stubs allow you to test your program in stages. For example, your first version of the procedure that evaluates a formula might be

```
(define evaluate-formula
  (lambda (...)
    (format #t "evaluate-formula~%")
    0))
```

This procedure only gives the correct answer if the correct answer is 0, but it does let you test code that calls `evaluate-formula`, e.g., the main program. This version of `evaluate-formula` is therefore a stub that will be replaced by the real thing when it is ready.

By doing things this way, you will arrange to test only one procedure at a time (when you start, everything is a stub). As you get one procedure working, you can replace another stub procedure with the real thing. This approach substantially reduces (though, unfortunately, it doesn't eliminate) the chances of an error that you can't immediately locate.

Detecting the end of file

How do you know whether you have read everything from a file? At the end of each file is a magic object called an "End Of File (eof) Object." Scheme places that object there; you don't have to. You can test to see whether you have read the eof object as follows:

```
(let ((form (read)))
  (if (eof-object? form)
      ...
```

To read all the elements in a file, use a procedure like this:

```
> (with-input-from-file "foo.bar"
    (lambda ()
      (letrec
        ((getem (lambda (form)
                  (if (eof-object? form)
                      '()
                      (cons form (getem (read)))))))
        (getem (read)))))
(hello world!)
```

Managing a software project

How do you organize the development of a large program? The key idea is to be in control of the process at each step. The best way to start is, of course, early. But if you make a plan, you will significantly enhance your chances of finishing successfully.

The key thing to remember is that **things take longer than you expect them to**. Always plan your time so that you will have something to hand in if you find you can't make any more progress.

Also, keep in mind that marathon hacking sessions are extremely unproductive. If you get stuck on one bug, simply get a printout of what's going wrong, and then start working on something else. It's surprising how often, once you get away from the computer and read that printout, you'll find the bug almost right away.

Remember to make backups of your project. Each time you get a piece working, save the file under a different name. (After you're finished, you can delete all but the final version.) This way, if you screw up one version, you can go back to the previous one. Use systematic names, e.g., `project1`, `project2`, and so on, so that you can locate backups quickly.

DELIVERABLES

1. the program's "main program", `mathematical-assistant`
2. a revised formula evaluator (which can be adapted from the spreadsheet lab)
3. a dialog that shows your program at work. Make sure that you demonstrate its correct evaluation of formulas, as well as its error handling features, such as reporting (and ignoring) invalid commands.

FOR FURTHER INVESTIGATION

1. Simplification is reducing a formula to an equivalent formula with fewer terms. For example, taking the derivative of x^2 gives you $1*x+1*x$, which is hardly the most readable output. It can be simplified to $2*x$. There are a number of rules that can help you simplify expressions:

   ```
   u*0 = 0
   u*1 = u
   u+0 = u
   u-0 = u
   u+u = 2*u
   u-u = 0
   ```

   Other rules can be added, if you feel like it. Beware of mathematical problems if you do: for example, it's ok to simplify x/x to 1, but only provided that you know that $x \neq 0$.
   We want a procedure (`simplify formula`), much like the derivative procedure, that simplifies expressions. Hook it in so that derivatives are displayed in a simplified format.
2. Add numeric integration (don't even *think* of symbolic integration!). Refer to Lab 9 for methods of doing integration (the trapezoidal rule is perfectly adequate), and add an `integrate` command: (`integrate formula low high step`). The meaning of this is to integrate *formula* from *low* to *high* using step size *step*.

Deliverables:

1. a listing of `simplify` and a printout showing it working as part of the math assistant
2. a listing of `integrate` and examples, showing that the system can numerically integrate `sqrt` between 0 and 10, for a variety of step sizes

Lab 31

Using the Query System

OBJECTIVES

This lab familiarizes you with QScheme rules by asking you to write a a set of QScheme rules for a problem. In the process, you will see the strengths of rule-based programming, and some of the limitations of QScheme.

WHAT YOU NEED TO KNOW

Read up through the end of Chapter 10.

PROBLEM STATEMENT

Consider carefully the following explanation of the way that Virtually Real Software, Ltd., is organized.

There are exactly two kinds of employees at VRS: programmers and managers, though an employee can be both a programmer and a manager. The president is a manager, as are Mary and Jacques. Bill and Ben know the same languages that Leon knows. Anyone who knows one of the programming languages Scheme, Lisp, Smalltalk, or C++ is a programmer. Lois knows Lisp. David knows Scheme. Leon has written a program in C++. Bill is the accountant at VRS. Lisp and Scheme are so similar that anyone who knows Lisp knows Scheme. Hanna, the president of VRS, knows Lisp.

Hanna manages Mary. Mary manages Bill, Jacques, and Leon. Jacques manages Ben, Lois, and David.

First you need to write a set of QScheme rules that express the above information. Make your rules as similar as possible to the above explanation, i.e., don't put anything in the rules that isn't in the explanation. Just take each sentence and, if possible, make one or more rules out of it. Note: there may be other things you know about computers, programming languages, companies, or other things that are not stated above. Do *not* put these facts in your rules.

You need to write the following as QScheme queries:

1. Is Lois a programmer?
2. Who knows Scheme?
3. Who are the programmers?
4. Who are the managers?
5. Is Bill an employee?

We also want a QScheme query to find out what languages Leon knows. You will find that you can't answer this question given the rules you have built. Write an additional rule (*not* a rule that says that Leon knows Smalltalk!) which can be used to answer this question.

What if we wanted to determine whom Hanna manages? The simplest way to write a new rule for this is to state that "a manages b if a manages c and c manages b". This lets the chaining system connect two facts. If you are using a forward chainer, this works perfectly. But qscheme uses backward chaining. In this case, to solve (manages Hanna ?x) might lead to an infinite loop! To deal with this problem using a backward chainer, we break recursive rules, such as manages, into two parts: a first part that examines a fact, such as "Mary manages Bill" and a second part that recurses. We'll need a new rule such as indirectly-manages. If A manages B, then A indirectly manages B (so that it means by 0 or more intermediate managers).

BEFORE THE LAB

1. Prepare a set of rules that expresses the first paragraph of information about VRS Ltd.
2. Prepare a QScheme query for each of the numbered questions about VRS. Write down the answer you expect for each of your queries.
3. Write down the rules that tell us what languages Leon knows.
4. Write down the rules that express the new information about `manages` to the rules.
5. Prepare a recursive rule that finds out who manages whom, either directly or indirectly. Write down a query that determines whom Mary manages, either directly or indirectly.

CHECKPOINT

1. Write the following in predicate logic: "Everyone who does this lab learns."
2. Write the logic statement in the previous line as a rule.
3. Is Leon a programmer?

DURING THE LAB

1. Type in your rules, and get a printout of them. (The Scheme form you prepare should be a definition of a variable called `myrules`.) Check it over carefully to make sure that it's correct.
2. Load the goodie `qscheme.scm`.
3. For each of the queries you have written, try it with your rule set, and check to make sure you got the answer you had anticipated. If not, perhaps your rules is incorrect: check it over, and make any needed correction. Once you have all the queries query working, produce a printout (of the queries and the responses from QScheme), and put it aside.
4. Add the new rules about direct management, including the recursive rules about indirect management. Find out who Mary manages, either directly or indirectly.

DELIVERABLES

1. the printout of the rules
2. the printout the queries and the results
3. the new rules that help us answer questions about who manages whom
4. the results of the new queries

FOR FURTHER INVESTIGATION

We can establish the connection between a set of rules and a database system, to use the strengths of both. We have mentioned that the query system and the data base manager are intended to work together: if the query system can't answer a query, e.g., (has-taken joe ma12), it can look in a table named has-taken. The easiest way to do this is to keep an association list, or *alist*, of tables, in which the cars are symbols, e.g.,

```
( (has-taken . <has-taken table>) ...)
```

Study the code for `forward`, the forward chaining version of the query system and see how to add this feature. (Note: the table alist can reasonably be stored in a global variable.) The code appears in Chapter 10 of the text and in the `fqscheme.scm` goodie. We have designed the query system so that this should be a fairly straightforward process, if you read the code carefully enough. Don't expect to understand everything about the query system in order to do this lab; just try to find the place where QScheme handles facts, and modify that code.

Because of the way the forward chainer works, including table information is grossly inefficient. Explain why. Usually we would use database information in backward chaining, but the code for the backward chainer is complex, so we are using the forward chainer.

While you're at it, also prepare a knows table that shows who knows which programming language (this will only include knows facts, not rules that let us conclude that somebody knows something).

Now make your modifications to the query system so as to interface it to the data base system (in the goodie dbscheme.scm). Load both goodies into Scheme and test them out. Don't make any changes to the data base system. Modify your rules so as to delete all facts (but not rules) about who knows which programming language, and add to it the knows table, and save the modified version under the name myrules2.scm. Now try it out, and get a printout.

Deliverables: a listing of the modification to the appropriate part of fqscheme.scm, the knows table, and a transcript that shows the query system working with the database system, using the knows table

Lab 32
Assembly-Language Programming

The Gleam machine shows how real machines evaluate expressions by moving data into and out of registers, and operating on values in registers. In addition, gap lets you write procedures for the Gleam machine. This lab asks you to write procedures in gap, including tail-recursive procedures.

WHAT YOU NEED TO KNOW

Read Chapter 11 up through Section 11.3. Make sure you are familiar with gap programming, Gleam instructions, and how to call and return from procedures in gap.

PROBLEM STATEMENT

We will design and implement a series of gap procedures. Each in turn will use more advanced assembly language programming ideas. Use the register conventions describe in Chapter 11 while writing the procedures.

Conditionals

We want to write a gap program to express:

```
(define compute
  (lambda (foo bar baz)
    (if (> foo bar)
        (* baz foo)
        (* bar foo)))))
```

The gap code should expect the values of foo, bar, and baz to be in registers 4, 5, and 6. The result should be in register 7. To test your code you will need a program that loads values into registers 4, 5, and 6. The program calls compute and prints out the result (in register 7).

Characters

In Chapter 3 we designed a procedure to determine whether a character is a vowel. That procedure used char-ci? to test character equality. We'll simplify things by using char=?.

```
(define vowel?
  (lambda (ch)
    (or
      (char=? ch #\a)
      (char=? ch #\e)
      (char=? ch #\i)
      (char=? ch #\o)
      (char=? ch #\u))))
```

We want to translate vowel? into gap. Assume that ch is in register 5. The result should be in register 6. In order to test your gap version of vowel?, you'll need to design some test inputs and a program like your compute tester, to load values, call vowel?, and print the returned result.

Remember that Gleam has no special representation for characters. They are just an interpretation of certain integer values.

Strings

We need a gap procedure `strlen` that counts the number of characters in a string. We will implement a string as a sequence of memory locations, each containing a character code, terminated by a location that contains a negative integer. We could write this in Scheme as:

```
(define strlen
  (lambda (mem loc)
    (letrec
      ((help
        (lambda (i len)
          (if (< (vector-ref mem i) 0)
            len
            (help (add1 i) (add1 len))))))
      (help loc 0)))))
```

In your gap code, `strlen` will take one argument, `loc`, the initial location in the string, in register 5.

BEFORE THE LAB

1. Design your `compute` procedure and its tester program. Write down your test inputs.
2. Design your `vowel?` procedure and its tester program. Are there any inputs that will cause `vowel?` to produce an error?
3. Design your `strlen` procedure and its tester program. Make sure that your tests include all the important cases.

PITFALLS AND ADVICE

Comment your code while you are writing it, line by line. You will be better able to understand it later; moreover, comments will be a real help during debugging. You should test small blocks of code so that you understand their effect.

There are many errors you may run across while programming gap.

- The initial values produced by the `dataword` directive must all be integers. The line `p (dataword #t)` will cause gap to print:
  `Error in assemble: value #t not a number.`
  You can fix it by replacing the Boolean value with an integer: `p (dataword 1)`—in gap *true* is anything but 0.
- Gleam/2 instructions are not available in Gleam/1.

  `(display 6)`
  `Error in control-unit: Illegal opcode 206.`

  Use `(outnum 6)` instead.
- If you use a symbolic name for a location that has not been defined:

  `one not defined`
  `Error: Source 2 at 6     one`

- You cannot output a value. You must load the value into a register.

  `(outchar #\i)`
  `Error in <: #\i is not a real number.`

  The second problem here is that characters in Gleam are represented as integer codes.
- The assembler directive is `define-symbols`.

  `from (define-symbol (one . 1)`
  `Error: Opcode at 0     define-symbol`

  This further generates the error:

```
Error in <: (one . 1) is not a real number.
```

that can be fixed by using (define-symbols (one . 1) ...

- If you have defined i and j as locations, and then try to output the values at those locations, gap will complain:

```
(outnum i)
..
(outnum j)
Register out of range 17
Register out of range 18
```

Gleam is trying to use the location addresses as register numbers. Remember that the location numbering system is independent of the register numbering system.

- If the labels i and j have not been defined, you will get the following messages:

```
Error: Address label at 0    i
Error: Address label at 5    j
```

CHECKPOINT

1. How does gap represent *true* and *false*?
2. What is wrong with the instruction (load 0 100 16)?
3. Under what conditions will the sequence:

```
(inchar 5)
(load 6 num)
(mpy 5 5 6)
```

cause an error, assuming you enter a character?

DURING THE LAB

1. Load the goodie gleam.scm.
2. Define your gap program:

```
> (define myprog
  '(
    (define-symbols (r4 . 4) ....
```

3. To assemble the program:

```
> (assemble myprog)
Locations used: 12
done
> (go)
00
Execution terminated.
```

gap informs you of the number of memory locations used. (go) starts up the program at location 0. The program prints 00. Then gap indicates that it has executed halt by typing Execution terminated.

If your program goes into an infinite loop, stop it as you would any Scheme program. If you restart your gap program without assembling it, you may find odd results, since the program may have altered memory cells, including locations that are part of the program.

trace-gleam is a flag that causes each instruction that is executed to produce a trace line, showing what is being executed, if it is #t. This will produce a *lot* of output. It defaults to #f.

4. Enter your compute procedure and test it on a variety of inputs.

5. Define your `vowel?` procedure and try it out on a series of inputs. How will you show your inputs and outputs?

6. Define your `strlen` procedure and try it out on a series of inputs.

AFTER THE LAB

You could simplify the `vowel?` procedure by using indexing, and storing the vowels in a particular manner. Outline briefly how you would do so, and show which `gap` instructions you would use to access the table of vowels.

DELIVERABLES

1. a listing of your `compute` program (the procedure plus its testing program) and a listing of the testing session showing that it works

2. the `vowel?` program and its tests

3. the `strlen` program and its tests

4. the answer to the "After the Lab" question